IT'S
NOT
JUST
YOU

» IS SOMETHING WRONG WITH ME? I'M NOT WHO EVERYONE THINKS I AM. DO OTHER WOMEN FEEL LIKE THIS? (AM I CRAZY?) MAYBE IT'S JUST ME. I THINK I NEED HELP— NOT THAT I COULD TELL ANYONE! I CAN'T JUST STOP. I ALWAYS TELL MYSELF, "GIRL, YOU ARE OUT OF CONTROL." HOW DID IT GET THIS FAR? I CAN'T KEEP THIS UP! I WONDER, IS THERE ANY HOPE FOR ME? ASHLEY CHESNUT

Freeing Women to Talk about Sexual Sin and Fight It Well

B&H
PUBLISHING
NASHVILLE, TENNESSEE

Published by B&H Publishing Group
Nashville, Tennessee

Dewey Decimal Classification: 155.3
Subject Heading: SEX (PSYCHOLOGY) /
SEX ROLES / SEXUAL ETHICS

Cover design by B&H Publishing Group.
Author photo by Caroline Elizabeth Film.

For my small group girls past and present.
It has been a privilege to journey alongside you and
grow together as followers of Jesus. This book is one
of the many ways God has used you in my life—and now
in the lives of others, and His work isn't finished.
To Him be the glory.

CONTENTS

PART 3—How to Fight Against Sexual Sin

APPENDIX

Introduction

"DO YOU REMEMBER A COUPLE OF WEEKS AGO WHEN I MEN-tioned not feeling close to God?"

The college student sitting in front of me—we'll call her Phoebe—took a deep breath before continuing, "I know we talked through several reasons for why this could be, but unconfessed and unrepentant sin—that's it. *That's* why I haven't felt close to God."

Then she looked around to make sure others couldn't hear, and her voice dropped to a whisper as she revealed, "I struggle with masturbation!"

I vaguely remember her sinking back into the booth, relieved to finally get the words out, but she also nervously gazed at me, waiting on my response. Internally, I begged God to answer my James 1 prayer for wisdom because I had no idea what to say or do next.

As you can imagine, I did not anticipate our conversation taking *that* particular turn, but it was a huge moment for both of us. For her, it marked a point in her spiritual growth of con-fessing sin and pursuing holiness in *all* areas of her life. For me, that conversation launched me into the deep end of the pool of discipleship, and little did I know that the next month would plunge me deeper still.

The next conversation happened a couple of days later in the same college food court but with a different girl—we'll call her "Whitney." She quickly jumped right in with her confession, ready to free herself of a secret. It turns out that Phoebe had shared her struggle with masturbation with one of her friends—Whitney—only to learn that Whitney shared the same struggle!

Over the next couple of weeks, I discovered that many of the young ladies I discipled were dealing with sexual sin, some to an addiction level. By the end of the semester, I felt like I'd experienced spiritual whiplash from all the confessions of sexual sin. I had no idea that masturbation was such a common struggle among women. Furthermore, most of the gals I discipled attended a Christian university, and they came across as good church girls. The more conversations I had, though, the more I discovered that these "good church girls"—along with many of their friends, sorority sisters, and family members—were entrenched in sexual sin, particularly masturbation.

For the next three years, these women and I embarked on a journey of learning how to battle against sexual sin and how to deal with sin's shrapnel. When they graduated, I thought I would get a reprieve from such a grueling season. God had done mighty things in their lives, for which I was incredibly grateful. But I was exhausted.

At the end of that summer, I began a new college small group, and I naively thought we'd begin with basic topics such as how to study the Bible and how to share the gospel. But within one week, I had five young women from our church seek me out to confess their sexual sin and to ask for help. Some of them had full-blown addictions, and I felt like I'd yet again been tossed into the trenches.

The first go-round three years earlier, I didn't know what to expect when discipling women who struggle with sexual sin, but this time, I knew more of what I was signing up for. But knowing what's coming doesn't spare us from the very real weight, difficulty, and exhaustion of actually going through that thing when it comes. Eventually my body felt the stress of this second go-round, and within a month, I contracted shingles.

Fast-forward to the present day where I serve as the associate director of my local church's young adult ministry. God continues to bring women with all sorts of sexual struggles into my life, and through the past decade of ministry experience, I've learned some things. For instance, many women don't know *why* sexual sin—such as masturbation—is sin. Did you know that some women continue engaging in sexual sin because they're afraid of the pain they'll face if they stop and examine why they do it in the first place? I also regularly encounter women who struggle with sexual sin and have checked all the boxes of things that should help them resist temptation (i.e., reading their Bible, praying, memorizing Scripture, having accountability, etc.), but they still find themselves giving into the same sin over and over. They don't know why or how to stop, and their situation feels hopeless.

Through my years of working with women, I've observed that sexual sin isn't just a male struggle, nor is it specifically a college girl struggle, teenage struggle, singles' struggle, or middle-age struggle. This is a struggle for *women of all ages and life stages*, but more often than not, it remains a secret struggle. Such secrecy breeds shame and isolation, leading women to battle sexual sin alone and to believe the lie that "it's just me."

Not only has God continued to bring struggling women my way, He also provided the opportunity to go back to school for biblical counseling training in order to be more equipped as a disciple-maker. When that first round of confessions occurred, I searched for every resource I could find on the topics of sexuality, sexual sin, and sex addiction, and I became discouraged at the lack of resources specifically addressing sexual sin *and women*.

Much of what I did find, particularly about masturbation, was directed to men. I can remember giving one such book to a girl who read it and returned it to me, voicing her frustration that the author hadn't acknowledged that women struggle with this too. She told me that this only added to the shame she felt for being a female struggling with what this Bible teacher presented as a "male" sin.

Since I encountered a lack of resources specifically for women, I sought the counsel of mature believers. I studied my Bible like I'd never studied it before, and oh, how I was driven to my knees in prayer for these women and for myself! Over and over again, God was faithful, and His Spirit was at work in me and in the women I've labored with and ministered to over the years.

There's so much I didn't know then that I know now. What I didn't expect in all of this was how God would grow *me* as I journeyed with the women He'd placed in my life. My former pastor David Platt commonly remarks how God "has this thing rigged." We think we're discipling and helping others only to realize how He is using them—the very people we're "helping"—to grow, develop, and sanctify *us*.

God has used these years of ministry—these women—to teach me some important things, including how to distinguish between symptoms of sin and their root. I also learned humility and dependence on the Lord as I realized my inadequacy and how my own sin struggles make me just as broken and in need of God's grace. I learned how sanctification truly is a lifelong process that happens one day and one choice at a time, and I've seen how God truly can change lives, redeem brokenness, and empower us to live in freedom and holiness.

I won't lie—there are days where the trenches of fighting sin are a hard place to be. Days where you're tired of the struggle. Days where the dailyness of the battle is wearisome. Days where you feel so dirty because you see the grotesqueness of your sin and how pervasive it is in your life. Days where it's all you can do to put one foot in front of the other. Days where you see the pain you and those around you are experiencing and you just want to weep over the carnage of sin in this world. Days where you wonder if the war will ever end and if you'll survive it with your faith intact.

But since that first confession in that college food court so many years ago, I have seen the beauty of the gospel and the sufficiency of my Savior. I have seen God's design for His church and how we as believers need each other and are not meant to live the Christian life alone. I have experienced God's grace in the trenches and am continuously reminded that we as Christians fight against sin from a position of victory because of Christ.

I don't know what led you to pick up this book. Maybe you struggle with sexual sin. Or maybe you're like I was with my first college small group—feeling unequipped and unprepared to help the people God has placed in your life. The book you're holding is what I wish I'd had all those years ago, and I pray it equips you in your journey. More than anything, I pray it points you to Christ and the hope we have in Him.

To give you a sense of what's ahead, Part 1 explains *why* we sin, particularly in the area of sexuality. Part 2 clarifies *what* God's design for sex is, so you can grasp why sexual sin is sin. And once you understand *why* you're broken and *what* God's design for sex is, Part 3 helps you know *how* to respond, giving you practical tools for fighting sexual sin in your life. (Appendices in the back of the book also explore the issues of sex addiction, sexual abuse, and trauma.)

Whatever form sexual struggles take in your life—whether you're in the trenches yourself or walking with a struggler—I pray this book opens your eyes to the truth that *it's not just you*. You're not the only one battling your particular brand of sin. You're not the only female, and you're not the only

Christian. You're also not alone as you battle, for you have a Savior who is always with you and who doesn't tire of you or get annoyed with you. He compassionately cares for His children, and through His Word, God teaches us what "healthy and whole" was always supposed to look like and how we can help each other love and follow Him.

To God be the glory.

>> **CHAPTER 1** <<

Our Sexual Brokenness

I KNEW WE NEEDED TO TALK ABOUT IT.

Conviction wasn't my problem. My problem was that I didn't know what to say or how to say it. When you're three or four months out from a speaking engagement, that's an okay problem to have. But as the mental block continued and as the countdown for the event dropped from months to weeks to days, my anxiety (and prayer life) dramatically increased.

What did the ladies in our church's Singles 20s/30s Ministry need to hear on the topic of sexuality? I knew some of the girls' stories, but I didn't know them all. What sexual sins were the most prevalent? What misconceptions did they have?

My working assumption was not *if* our ladies struggled with sexual sin but *how many*. I felt like teaching on this topic was akin to opening a can of worms; however, it's a can of worms that the church needs to open.

That was by far the most difficult talk I've ever had to prepare, and I agonized about it for weeks. As part of that teaching series, those who came completed an anonymous sexual survey. Seventy-four single women in their twenties and thirties completed this survey and reported:

- 23% had engaged in premarital or extra-marital sex
- 11% had sexted in the last two years
- 14% had engaged in oral sex in the last two years
- 14% had struggled with same-sex attrac-tion at some point in their life with two women reporting that they currently struggle with it
- 19% disclosed that they'd been raped or sexually abused
- 31% had intentionally sought out porn at some point in their life
- 19% had intentionally viewed porn in the last six months with one woman saying she views it at least once a week
- 70% had masturbated at some point in their life
- 51% admitted that masturbation is cur-rently a struggle (frequency varied widely with 20% masturbating at least once a month and 9% masturbating at least once a week)

The War We're Not Winning and How Our Silence Is Costing Us the Battle

While there are many takeaways from a survey like this, it demonstrates the prevalence of sexual brokenness. (And if you're wondering why I refer to these things as "brokenness," stick with me. We'll get there.) On one hand, I was surprised by the results; on the other hand, I wasn't surprised at all. In fact, some of the numbers were lower than I anticipated. But here's what did shock me—their responses when I asked what topics *they had not heard biblical teaching on.*

- Thirty percent had not heard biblical teaching on pornography. That's nearly one of every three women who were surveyed!
- Fifty-five percent had not heard biblical teaching on masturbation, which is roughly one in two women. (I was actually surprised by how many *had* heard teaching on this subject!)
- Seventy-seven percent had not heard biblical teaching on oral sex. That's seven out of ten women.
- Forty-five percent (a little less than half the women) had not heard biblical teaching on cohabitation. (So more had heard teaching on porn than on living together before marriage.)
- Twenty-two percent had not heard biblical teaching on homosexuality or same-sex attraction. That's two out of ten women.

These numbers surprised me. What do these numbers say about us as a church—both my local church and the "capital c" Church? Our singles ministry is a revolving door of people. Only a few of our folks actually grew up in our city, so these statistics represent what a plethora of churches, youth groups, and college ministries have and have not taught. While some of these ladies did not grow up in church, the majority did—and in the Bible Belt!

The church's silence surprised me. If we're not bringing light to the darkness, then we're contributing to it, and often, it's our silence that allows the darkness to continue. If we're not talking about sexual sin, then we're allowing it to grow unchecked in our people. Our silence is our complicity.

Sure, it's not comfortable to talk about sexual sin. Do you think I *enjoy* talking with women about masturbation? But it's essential to provide biblical teaching if we want to equip our people to follow Christ in their daily lives, especially in an age of sexual atheism in the church where self-proclaimed Christians disregard the authority of God in the areas of their sexual identity and sexual choices.

What We All Have in Common

For men and women alike, sin touches *every* area of our lives, including our sexuality. This means sexual sin has affected *you* in some way, just like it has me. Maybe you're the victim of someone's unwanted sexual attention. Maybe you gave your consent. Maybe you slept with someone last night. Or maybe you haven't ever kissed anyone but have had lustful thoughts about someone, watched a sex scene on TV, listened to raunchy music lyrics, dressed for attention, or laughed at a perverted joke. Whatever its form, sexual sin affects us all.

Now, hear me out. I'm not saying these things to condemn you. I'm saying these things because starting here creates a sense of humility and helps us approach the topic of sexual sin as fellow strugglers. We all struggle in different ways and to different degrees, but we're all sinners. We're all broken, and we're all *sexually* broken. *It's not just you.*

In 1 Corinthians 10:13, Paul writes: "No temptation has come upon you except what is common to humanity." While the sin may vary, the temptation itself is *common*. The craving to cope and to satisfy ourselves is something we all experience, even if we do that in different ways. Your battle may look different from those around you, but we're all fighting the same enemy in the same war, which we are insufficient to do on our own. Thankfully, we hope in the same Savior who has already defeated sin and who promises to help us in our fight.

What Is Broken Was Once Whole

The very fact that we would say something is broken requires that, at one time, it was whole. While you have been a sinner since conception (Ps. 51:5), the human race did exist once without sin, and Genesis 3 tells the story of how humanity willingly chose to move from God's good design into brokenness. But before looking at why we're broken, it's helpful to examine how we were made and how restoration is coming because of Christ.

Growing up in church, I heard all the Bible stories you'd expect: Noah and the Flood, Jonah and the whale, David and Goliath, etc. But it wasn't until my early twenties that I realized all these seemingly random Bible stories aren't so random after all. They're all contributing to an overarching storyline. It's like how *Captain America, Thor, Black Panther,* and the other Marvel movies each tell separate stories, but these separate movies are all connected to tell one bigger story.

The Bible tells one bigger story, and it happens in four acts, sort of like a play. A snapshot of this big storyline can be summed up in four words: creation, fall, redemption, and consummation.

Creation: Genesis 1–2 presents a world that God created without sin. He made people in His image, meaning they reflect Him and represent Him in the world, and at this time, all of creation was at peace with God and with each other, flourishing in His good design.

Fall: Brokenness occurred with the Fall in Genesis 3 as Adam and Eve disobeyed God's command and rebelled against His authority. This choice resulted in physical and spiritual death for all of humanity, introducing sin to the world (Rom. 5:12). While people are still image-bearers of God, sin mars the image, and while many Bible stories (especially in the Old Testament) seem like bizarre scenes from reality TV, Scripture demonstrates over and over the devastating effects of sin on creation and on our relationship with God and one another.

Redemption: All of humanity stands separated from God because of sin, and we can do nothing on our own power to resolve the situation. We can't be good enough because we're compromised on the inside, meaning we *can't* be perfect. We would have to satisfy *every* demand of God's law and keep *every* command in order to be righteous (Gal. 3:10–14). Therefore, any attempt to earn God's favor and salvation is insufficient to please the just, holy, and righteous God of the universe.

God knew Adam and Eve would sin, and in His infinite wisdom, though they betrayed Him, He made a way for humanity to be reconciled to Himself. He did this by sending His Son Jesus Christ to be born as a man, to live a sinless life on this earth, to die on a cross, and to rise from the dead. He had to be a man in order to be eligible to be our substitute just as a relief pitcher in baseball must be an actual pitcher in order to be an effective substitute (Heb. 2:17). He had to be sinless because only *perfect* sacrifices are acceptable to God (Heb. 9:11–10:18). He had to die because "the wages of sin is death" (Rom. 6:23), and He had to rise from the dead in order to defeat sin and death and to enable us to rise from the dead and have eternal life with Him (1 Cor. 15:12–58; John 11:25–26).

Though we've been running up a tab of sin, if we turn from our sin and trust in Christ as our Lord and Savior, God applies Jesus' perfection and death to our tab. Even though we are guilty of sin, God the Judge declares that we are not guilty and that, instead, we are righteous. God pardons us from our offenses because Christ took our punishment and guilt, and He can call us righteous because He looks at us through the blood of His Son. This is how God can accept us while we remain sinners, enabling us to go from God's enemies to members of His family.

Consummation: In the timeline of salvation history, we currently live between redemption and consummation. God is moving all of creation toward restoration. What is broken will one day be made whole. This restoration will occur when Christ returns, and at this time, He will usher in the new heaven and the new earth, which will be void of sin and all of its effects (Rev. 20:7–21:8). Because of Christ's death and resurrection, those who trust in Him for salvation are made new (2 Cor. 5:17), but in the consummation era of salvation history, *all of creation* will be made new.

For those who are Christians, we already experience Christ's transformation of our lives, adoption into His family, and the indwelling of the Holy Spirit, but we are not yet experiencing all the benefits that await us at the consummation. While God sees us as righteous, we still experience the effects of sin's presence in the world. This is what it means to live as Christians in the tension of the "already-not yet" timeline of history. While we as Christians have been redeemed by Christ, we wait for the day when God will renew all of creation, restoring the universe to the peace and sinlessness that was experienced back in the garden. This good news of what's to come offers us hope as we live in the brokenness of daily life here on earth.

Creation, Fall, redemption, and consummation—that's it. That's the storyline of the Bible, and it provides a whole lot of answers and insight into the problem of our sexual brokenness, as you'll see in chapter 2.

CHAPTER 2

Why We're Broken: Part I

YOU WOULDN'T BE READING THIS BOOK IF YOU DIDN'T KNOW there was brokenness in the world and in you. There's brokenness because we've been sinned against, and there's brokenness because we've sinned in response. We're fallen people in a fallen world. But God compassionately responds to our brokenness, for as one preacher puts it, Scripture "defines God's mercy at the same time that it reveals human need."[1] God offers hope and redemption, and we must bear this in mind as we delve into the reasons for sexual brokenness in our world.

If you're like me, you prefer good news to bad news, and you might be tempted to skim (or skip!) the next section about our brokenness and sin and head straight to the good news of God's mercy and grace—but don't do it. Why? Because understanding *how* we're broken and *why* sin is deemed "sin" will enable us to better fight against it. Sin is only effectively treated if we deal with it at the root instead of focusing solely on the fruit, and the following sections describe the root. Hang with me in this. Some of what I say might be hard to hear, and things will get grim before they get better. (But they *will* get better.) So take a deep breath and keep reading.

Our Sinfulness

We Are All Wicked

At one point in the conversation, I asked if she was a masochist.

That was my sardonic response to a girl (who we'll call Lucy) informing me that she would, on a weekly basis, have sex with a guy before driving over to meet with her small group *that was doing a study on sin!*

Another girl—Sadie—visited our church with a friend, and in our first conversation, Sadie nonchalantly talked about her boyfriend sleeping over at her place. Normally, Christians—even cultural Christians—in the Bible Belt wouldn't openly admit this sort of thing at church because they know it goes against what the Bible teaches. But Sadie didn't seem to recognize her living situation as a problem.

In Luke 6:43–45, Jesus teaches that a tree is known by its fruit, meaning that our behavior indicates what we truly believe. With both Lucy and Sadie, their sexual choices—their fruit—wasn't their primary problem. Their disobedience to God in this area of their life reflected their beliefs about God. Maybe they don't know God as their Savior, or maybe they don't fully understand how the gospel applies to daily life. With this in mind, I focused a follow-up conversation with Sadie on what she believed about God rather than on her sexual behavior. When I asked her if she considered herself a Christian, she replied: "I don't know. I'm not sure."

At this point, she'd heard the gospel multiple times—both at church and at small group, but I went through everything again, explaining the gospel. And here's the strange part: while Sadie agreed with all the things we discussed and got the gospel on a principle-level, she expressed an unwillingness to surrender to Christ's lordship in the areas of guys and sex. On a positive note, Sadie grasped that being a Christian means obeying God in this area of her life. She saw the fruit of her life and knew it didn't match the root of a Christ-follower. Even though she went to church and even joined a Bible study group, she knew her life didn't reflect trusting in Christ as *Lord*.

Do you identify with Lucy or Sadie? Do you find yourself going to church or a Bible study group while simultaneously giving into sexual sin? If so, it's likely you feel torn about this or even crazy for continuing to do both, especially if you're around Bible-believing Christians who call sin what it is. Do you wonder why you keep coming back to church or your godly friends, especially since it just adds to your feelings of guilt and shame?

It makes no sense apart from the Spirit's work inside of you. Typically, we avoid people or things that convict us or challenge how we want to live, so I'm encouraged when I encounter women like Lucy and Sadie because it's evident God is working in their lives to draw them to Himself. So if this is you, take heart. Maybe the reason you keep putting yourself in a position to learn more about God is because God is moving in your life. Maybe the reason why you're reading this book is because God wants to meet you where you are and help you.

If you're the person walking alongside a Lucy or a Sadie as her small group leader or friend, be encouraged that the Holy Spirit is working behind the scenes and has put you in her life to point her to God. Hopefully, you will encounter more people like this young woman—more sexual atheists (Christians as well as nonbelievers)—who are attracted to Christ in you. Our responsibility when we encounter sexually broken individuals is to listen to them, love them, and share how the gospel applies to them where they are. If they're unsaved, we explain the gospel's power to reconcile them to God. If they're saved, we show how the gospel that saved them gives them the motivation and the power to resist temptation in daily life.

Whether you're the sexual struggler or someone shepherding a struggler, we're all masochists when it comes to sin. We reap consequences of pain and shame as a result of our decision to sin and do what we want. We've all been Lucy or Sadie in our own way. We have all resisted Christ's Lordship of our lives, whether it involved sexual sin or some other category of sin. This shows how much we *all* need the gospel. I need it just as much today as I did before I became a Christian. While my standing before God has changed since becoming a Christian, I still have a sin nature and am tempted to sin on a daily basis. Why? Because I became a sinner at conception. As Psalm 51:5 states, "Indeed, I was guilty when I was born; I was sinful when my mother conceived me." Romans 5:12 further explains, "Therefore, just as sin entered the world through one man, and death through sin, in this way death spread to all people, because all sinned."

As these verses show, we are born into sin. When Adam and Eve ate the forbidden fruit, they introduced sin into the world and infected all of their descendants with a sin nature. As a result, "All have turned away; all alike have become corrupt. There is no one who does good, not even one."[2]

You might consider yourself a "good" person, but truthfully, you're not. Neither am I. You're a sinner, and so am I. All sin is against God, and His perfect character is what makes our offense so terrible and so worth the punishment of eternal separation from Him.

When you sin, you actively rebel against God. You are, in essence, turning to your Creator and telling Him He's not enough for you. That you know what's best for you. That you're wiser than Him. That your approach to sexuality and to life is better than His. Even if you don't say the words, you're communicating these things with your actions.

As Isaiah 53:6 says, "We all went astray like sheep; we all have turned to our own way; and the LORD has punished him

for the iniquity of us all." It's not just you. We were *all* born sinful and have, therefore, chosen our own way instead of God's
way, and that has consequences.

We Are All Weak

Earlier I mentioned a "sin nature." But what does that
mean? It means that, from birth, we are inclined away from
God toward sin. Romans 5:6 states, "For while we were still
weak, at the right time Christ died for the ungodly."[3] How does
the apostle Paul describe us? "Weak!"

If we weren't weak, we wouldn't struggle so much with
temptation. This truth became super evident as I walked alongside a particular girl—Jade—who had entered into a relationship that was toxic and sinful from the get-go. She acted out
sexually with the other person, and soon after, she confessed
her sin to her small group leaders and to me. But despite knowing the relationship was wrong, Jade kept returning to it.

One morning, I woke up to a text message from her saying
that she had been communicating with the other member of
the unhealthy duo. She did this despite knowing it was wrong,
despite the counsel she had received from everyone—and I
mean *everyone*—in her life, and despite the fact that no good
could come from it. Jade even acknowledged all of this, yet
she did it anyway. Why? Because she's weak. Just like you
and me.

Human weakness is one reason why Jesus taught us to
pray, "And lead us not into temptation, but deliver us from
evil."[4] Keep us from temptation because we're so weak we'd
give into it! When it comes to sin, we're like addicts. We can't
help ourselves. We keep giving into it, despite adverse consequences. Despite the fact that it backfires on us and wounds us
time and time again. This is why Jesus told Peter, James, and
John in the Garden of Gethsemane, "Watch and pray that you

may not enter into temptation. The spirit indeed is willing, but the flesh is weak."[5]

And if you're a leader looking down your nose at a woman struggling with sexual sin, let's hear from Paul, one of the Bible's leader of leaders, who tells us about his own weakness in Romans 7:

> For I do not understand what I am doing, because I do not practice what I want to do, but I do what I hate. . . . For the desire to do what is good is with me, but there is no ability to do it. For I do not do the good that I want to do, but I practice the evil that I do not want to do. . . . So I find this law at work: Although I want to do good, evil is right there with me. For in my inner being I delight in God's law; but I see another law at work in me, waging war against the law of my mind and making me a prisoner of the law of sin at work within me.[6]

Can I just say how thankful I am for Bible verses like this? I can read it and know I'm not the only one who feels frustrated—or at war—with myself. As this passage explains, there are two laws at work in us—one that loves God and one that loves sin. You may have a desire to do what's right, but your own proclivity toward sin will tempt you to disobey the God that you love. You might desire to obey Him, but at the same time, you might sense ungodly desires right next to the righteous ones! That doesn't make sin okay, but it does remind us that, while we strive to obey, we will not do so perfectly in this life. Again, we're weak. We're *all* weak.

WHY WE'RE BROKEN: PART I

Being Tempted Is *Not* a Sin

To clarify, being tempted is *not* a sin. The Bible clearly demonstrates this by stating that Jesus was tempted yet without sin: "For we do not have a high priest who is unable to sympathize with our weaknesses, but one who has been tempted in every way as we are, yet without sin."[7]

In light of this, being *tempted* to view porn, for example, is *not* a sin. Watching it or replaying it in our mind is.

Being *tempted* with same-sex attraction is *not* a sin. Giving into those thoughts and feelings or having an unhealthy relationship with someone of the same sex is.

Being *tempted* to masturbate is *not* a sin. Masturbating—or reading, watching, listening, or thinking about something to arouse yourself—is.

The Lord's Prayer is instructive here. In it, Jesus teaches us to pray: "forgive us our debts" but to "deliver us from evil."[8] So, Jesus tells us to ask forgiveness for our sin but to ask for deliverance from evil. Forgiveness and deliverance—those are two different actions. One indicates we're in the wrong; the other indicates that we need help.

We give permission for a tempting thought to linger in our mind. We imagine what it would be like to act on it, allowing scenarios to play out in our imagination, and before we know it, we're acting like David with Bathsheba, concocting some sort of plan to bring our fantasy into reality (see 2 Sam. 11:1–15)!

But here's what God promises: "No temptation has come upon you except what is common to humanity. But God is faithful; he will not allow you to be tempted beyond what you are able, but with the temptation he will also provide the way out so that you may be able to bear it."[9] God may not take the temptation away, but He *will* give us the strength to face it and resist it.

I'm reminded of a phone call I received from a girl after she had viewed porn (which meant starting over with her sobriety yet again). She reached out because she felt frustrated with herself and wanted encouragement. One of the things she expressed was how the temptation felt *relentless*. She couldn't seem to escape it or replace it. It was like a song stuck in her head that she could not get rid of (like "It's a Small World After All"). The tension mounted until she gave in. Giving in was one option to ending the temptation, but it wasn't effective. It wasn't God-honoring, and it wasn't the only option she had.

With this example, I also want to point out that temptation is a form of suffering. There's weariness that comes with fighting a battle that may last as long as you live. It can be painful to resist your desires. Plus, you experience spiritual warfare as you follow Christ. All of this to say, if you're being tempted, you're experiencing suffering. But going back to Scripture's promises, God is faithful to us in our temptation (1 Cor. 10:13), and He is with us when we are tempted. He provides a way of escape. He empowers us to resist and to flee, and He provides comfort to those who suffer (2 Cor. 1:3–4). These truths provide hope when we are tempted.

I'm often asked whether God will take away a particular struggle or if this is something a person will always experience this side of heaven. Paul's prayer in 2 Corinthians 12 is instructive here. He had a thorn of the flesh, and although we do not know what afflicted him, he petitioned God on three separate occasions to take it away. But what was God's response? "My grace is sufficient for you, for my power is perfected in weakness."[10]

God wouldn't take the thorn away, but He would provide grace and strength for Paul to bear with it. Paul intimately knew the truths he proclaimed in 2 Corinthians because he lived them. He knew that God was strong in his weakness because he witnessed it time and time again. He could proclaim God's sufficiency because he'd not only heard God's promise, he had experienced God fulfilling that promise.

Whether or not God takes away your temptation, He is still good, and He is still good to *you*. In our finite understanding, we will not always know the reasons why God would allow us to bear the burden of our particular sin struggle, but He does nothing without purpose. He works all things for the good of those who love Him (Rom. 8:28), but we will not recognize that good if we do not lean into Him.

In facing temptation, one must choose whether or not to deepen one's trust in the actual Savior or to turn to a functional savior. Do we love Him more than we love our sin? In moments of temptation, I find that asking myself that question and reminding myself of all that God has done for me prompts me to obey God rather than my desires.

Being Tempted Shows Us What We Worship

At one point in life, my dad tried to teach me to fish. (Notice I said "tried.") But fish are slimy when you pull them out of the water, and I just feel sorry for them as they're flapping about. And forget trying to remove the hook from their mouth—I just can't do it. It grosses me out, and I have no desire to try it again.

But that flapping fish gets caught because it goes after the bait that's on the hook. The fish sees the bait and wants it, and the desire for the bait leads the fish to pursue it. By the time the fish realizes it's in danger, it's too late. It's already hooked. This image is what James depicts when he says, "But each person is tempted when he is lured and enticed by his own desire."[11]

Temptation is enticing because it's attached to our desires. We're tempted by things we want. Maybe it's security, significance, attention, or affirmation, but because we want these things, we're tempted to procure them, even if it means acting in ways that do not glorify God. Paul David Tripp explains it this way: "Whatever rules the heart will exercise inescapable influence over the person's life and behavior."[12] What a person worships—*that's* what dictates their behavior. They cannot escape the influence of whatever it is that sits on the throne of their life.

For example, if my desire for security drives me, I will respond to situations that are out of my control by attempting to manipulate and manage what I can. This might mean that I become OCD about cleanliness, develop an eating disorder, or become a helicopter parent trying to control my child's life. I do this because security is what I crave, and I have allowed that to be what I ultimately treasure. But while I try to manage everything around me, at the end of the day, I cannot manage my own brokenness.

Whatever rules my heart—*that* is what I worship, and what I worship can be identified by what I love the most, fear the most, and desire the most.[13] Examine what those things are in your own life, and beware if your desire for someone or something is greater than your desire for God. You will give into temptation if your desires are not submitted to the lordship of Christ. You will be willing to manipulate circumstances to get what you want, and you will offend, hurt, lie, and more in order to obtain the object of your desire. All sin is a worship issue, so what are you worshiping? Is it the Lord?

Our sinfulness is the foundational reason for our brokenness, but it's not the only reason . . .

Our Wiring

Our brokenness stems from our sinfulness, but it can also be affected by our wiring, our genetic makeup. Deficiencies, diseases, and diagnoses exist because of the Fall, and what happens in and to our bodies affects us.

My mom once told me that people are like a table with four legs. There's a physical leg, an emotional leg, a spiritual leg, and a relational leg. When one of the legs isn't level, what happens to the table? It wobbles, right?

A person can have more than one table leg off at a particular time, so we should thoroughly examine our physical health in addition to our relationship with God, our relationships with others, and our emotional well-being. To get the table level again requires addressing each leg of the table. We must look at people holistically and recognize that an array of factors contributes to their struggles.

What's Sin and What's Sickness?

One human tendency is to blame our emotions and behavior on our biology. Looking at what addiction does to the brain can help us better understand this. As a person engages in the addictive behavior, their brain actually changes. Their actions affect their brain.

To understand this, we must grasp how the brain's reward system works. Prepare to nerd out with me for just a bit. I promise we'll come back to practical advice, but this stuff is really helpful to know.

When engaging in an activity that brings pleasure, a neurotransmitter called dopamine releases in the brain. Neurotransmitters are chemical messengers, and dopamine carries the message of *pleasure*. God has wired our brains to associate life-sustaining activities such as eating with pleasure, and in our brain, dopamine serves as a powerful motivator for behavior.

However, we can act in ways that abuse our own dopamine levels. When acting out, an addict overstimulates or floods their brain with dopamine at levels far beyond what is normally released when anticipating or enjoying other pleasures.

So now, whenever the addict even thinks about acting out, dopamine levels rise in the brain, which motivates the person to act on the thought.

As a person continues with their addictive behavior, their tolerance increases. Pleasure diminishes over time because they become used to it, which means novelty is needed in order to get the same dopamine fix as before. With porn addicts, this is how someone can go from viewing heterosexual porn to violent porn to child porn to acting out with prostitutes. The person needs to see different images or do different things in order to have a comparable level of dopamine flowing in the brain.

At this point, things that used to bring pleasure don't anymore because the level of pleasure they provide are normal levels not flood levels. "Normal" pleasure can't compare to "flood-level" pleasure, which contributes to why addicts choose their addiction over spouses, children, work, sleep, etc.

Essentially, addiction rewires the brain. Think of it as a dirt road. The more people drive down the dirt road, the more well-worn it becomes. The more people engage in the addictive activity, the easier it becomes to do it again because they're reinforcing those neuropathways in the brain. Therefore, addicts choose to sin, and their choices lead to bondage, resulting in the out-of-control behavior we associate with addiction.

Now, all of this has been about addiction. But as I reflect on my own sinful choices, I often consider what I'm doing to my brain.[14] What am I associating pleasure with? What neuropathway am I creating or reinforcing with my sinful choice?

If a dirt road isn't used in a while, it starts to grow over. Comparably, God has made our brains able to change. New neural pathways can be established, and unused ones can dissipate with time like old dirt roads. The technical term for this is the *neuroplasticity* of the brain.

However, these changes do not happen overnight. They take time and happen one choice at a time. Knowing all of this, God infused the Bible with commands to renew our minds and take thoughts captive (Rom. 12:2; Eph. 4:22–23; 2 Cor. 10:5). Because He knows that lingering on fleshly pleasures in our minds will entice us to act on them, He commands us to dwell on things that are true, honorable, just, pure, lovely, commendable, morally excellent, and worthy of praise (Phil. 4:8).

The more you choose to think and act a certain way, the more well-worn that pathway becomes, making it easier to choose the next time. Repetition causes structural changes in the brain. With this in mind, are you actively choosing the repetition of sinful thoughts and behaviors or the repetition of godly ones?

Sickness Does *Not* Excuse Sin

Why is it important to understand our wiring and its relationship to holiness and to sin? Because it affects how we view our situation. Do we blame God for a genetic predisposition that may exist? Do we understand how our own choices affect our body and our brains? Do we take personal responsibility for what is our own fault and trust God's sovereignty for what isn't?

In working with one girl who struggled with masturbation, I noticed that the way she talked about the temptation was different; her temptation seemed more intense, more painful, and more *physical.* So I asked her to start keeping a journal regarding her temptation. Through this, we identified that the intensity of her temptation aligned with her menstrual cycle. However, seeing a connection between her cycle and her sin did not give her permission to follow her body's impulses. Rather, knowing this pattern enabled her to better prepare for temptation at those times rather than be caught off guard by it.

Just because your biology may give you a propensity to sin does not mean you have an excuse to give into that sin. You don't get a pass because of your biology. Life is certainly more difficult as a result of physical or emotional issues, but these difficulties do not excuse sin. As Edward Welch states, "At most, biology is analogous to a friend who tempts us into sin. Such a friend might be bothersome, but he can be rebuked or resisted."[15]

While our biology does influence us, it does not determine our behavior. Our bodies do not make us sin; we *choose* to sin. We sin because of our own idolatry. But thankfully, our bodies cannot stop us from obedience; we can choose to trust and follow Jesus.

Ultimately, we can know that God gives "more grace" as James 4 states,[16] and His power is made perfect in our weakness. We can turn to God for the strength and the desire to trust and obey Him. Therefore, as Paul says in 2 Corinthians 4:16: "So we do not lose heart. Though our outer self is wasting away, our inner self is being renewed day by day."[17]

CHAPTER 3

Why We're Broken: Part 2

Our Woundedness

I know, I know. Another section of bad news about our brokenness.

As if our sinfulness and our wiring weren't enough, there's still two more contributing factors to discuss. But we're not without hope in any of this. We're not hopeless, no matter how broken we feel. However, to experience healing and comfort, we must adequately identify and understand the diagnosis in order to treat it. So with this in mind, let's examine a third reason for our brokenness: being wounded by others.

Several of the girls I've discipled come from dysfunctional families. One has a mom whose criticism of her looks, achievements, and decisions far outweighs the mom's affirmation of her. Another has a dad who is so controlling and manipulative that none of his children want a relationship with him. Another has parents whose behavior created an environment where she, the child, was made to feel emotionally responsible for them, and if she tried to do something they didn't like, they would berate her for being selfish and unloving in order to manipulate her into submission. Several have parents who have divorced or had affairs.

Does any of this sound familiar? Do you identify with any of these examples of woundedness? Some wounds are unintentionally inflicted by others with words being said or things happening to us that should not have occurred. Other wounds occur—not because of what was done but because of what *wasn't* done. Neglect. A father never telling you he loves you. A parent who wasn't present in your life, even though you lived in the same house. Or a parent who left—by overt choice or even by death.

The words and actions of others affect us. We've all been wounded to some degree, but the types of wounds and the depth of the woundedness will vary with each person. While we cannot change the fact that we've been wounded, we can choose how we respond.

In order to respond well, we need to first **assess the damage**. Because my South Georgia hometown is right off I-75 and only forty-five minutes from the Florida-Georgia line, whenever there's a hurricane in Florida, we prepare to open shelters for evacuees. The church I grew up in even held Red Cross trainings where folks in our community could get certified in various aspects of disaster relief and be ready to serve.

One such training I attended had to do with disaster assessment, which equipped us to enter a disaster area, evaluate the damage, and collect data, which we would communicate to the Red Cross. Before we could effectively begin addressing the disaster and especially before people could return to their homes and communities, we had to assess the damage. We had to identify possible issues with infrastructure and what local resources were still available.

What's been the damage in your own life? What hurts have you experienced? How has your environment shaped you?

To be clear, our environment is *not* determinative. It does not force us to act a certain way, but it *does* influence us. It affects us, but we have to take responsibility for how we respond. Being a victim does not mean that we get a pass and can live how we want, blaming our actions on others or on our past.

With assessing the damage in your life, I am *not* advocating that you wallow in the past. Think about looking at the past like a doctor looking at an X-ray or scan. Before doing surgery, a doctor will do a variety of tests or scans to determine the issue and what steps to take to address it. That's what we want to do with our past. We identify what our wounds actually are, so we can effectively address them. As Henry Cloud and John Townsend write in *Boundaries*, "God's desire is for you to know where your injuries and deficits are, whether self-induced or other-induced. Ask him to shed light on the significant relationships and forces that have contributed to your . . . struggles. The past is your ally in repairing your present and ensuring a better future."[1]

Our past can be viewed as our frenemy. It's our friend in that it helps us identify our injuries and deficits as Cloud and Townsend mention, and as we allow God to heal our memories, the past can point us to His sufficiency, goodness, and grace. Looking at God's faithfulness to us in the past can fortify our trust in Him in the present. But the past can also be our enemy if we do not allow God to heal it. We might suppress what's happened because we don't want to revisit the hurts, or we might want to hold onto our anger or resentment toward someone.

A fundamental reason why we should assess the damage is so we can **identify what lies we believe**. Because of what's happened, what do we believe about ourselves? About God? About others? One reason why we act the way we do is

because we think the way we do, which is why we must identify the thoughts and beliefs associated with our wounds.

One day as I walked to the church parking lot with a young
woman after a counseling conversation, I asked her to check
in with me that week to follow up on how she was doing, and
she actually said out loud (more to herself than to me), "I am
not a burden." She needed to hear herself say that she was
not being a burden to me by checking in as I'd asked. But she
spoke these words to herself because she often sees herself
as a burden. She's come to believe this of herself because of
wounds inflicted by her parents—the things they've said to
her and how they've treated her throughout her life.

Relatedly, what do you believe about what has happened
to you in your life? Do you think you're not enough? That
no one could love or accept you? That you're hopeless and
beyond help? Whatever lies you believe, they affect your view
of yourself, your relationship with God, and your relationship
with others. Lies keep us in chains.

Identifying our woundedness also helps us to **recognize
the many ways we have tried to manage our pain**. Most of the
time, I have no idea heading into a conversation that a girl is
going to spill her guts about her sexual sin. In one such conversation, it came out that the young woman was having oral sex
with someone—but her sexual sin was *not* the primary issue.

As we talked more about why this girl—Harper—was acting out, I learned about abuse that had occurred in her past.
I recognized that Harper did not know how to respond to
negative emotions in a healthy way. She had been stuffing her
emotions for years. She did not know how to cope, so in this
situation, Harper sought affirmation and attention from a guy
in order to confirm for herself that she was wanted and desired
by someone. To clarify, abuse is not always a reason for sexual sin, but if you're engaging in sexual sin, it's important to

examine why. If there's any woundedness or trauma in your story, that's helpful to acknowledge.

With regard to our woundedness, we have two response options: we either suppress them or allow God to heal them. Trying to forget what happened is like trying to hold a beach ball underwater. You can do it for a little while, but it's not sustainable. Eventually, the beach ball will get out from under you and pop up to the surface. This might take the form of an outburst of anger, a panic attack, etc., but your proverbial beach ball *will* surface if you do not address the areas of woundedness you have.

Regarding past hurts, H. Norman Wright puts it this way, "Our hurts from the past are like abscesses—raw, hemorrhaging wounds that become covered by scabs. But from time to time the scabs peel off. Unfortunately, what is uncovered is not the complete growth of restored life, but the same bleeding sore."[2]

What's the alternative? We either try to ignore that we have wounds, leaving them untreated, or we acknowledge that we have them and allow God to heal them. I once had a coworker with an infected wound on her leg, and because of the nature of the infection, the doctor had to reopen the wound and dig out the infected gunk in order for the wound to heal.

This is what must be done with the hurts from our past. Wounds need to heal properly. If they don't, they become infected. They get worse. And if we do not allow God to heal our wounds, we will become people who inflict wounds upon others.

Attempting to manage your own pain is *not* the same as it being transformed by God. How have you attempted to manage your woundedness? Have you sought to control your circumstances and relationships? Do you give people an emotional Heisman, not allowing them close enough to hurt you? Do you hold onto anger, stewing on past hurts and cultivating bitterness and resentment toward those who have caused you pain? Do you turn to substances, sleep, shopping, or food to comfort you?

What coping mechanisms have been your go-to? In what ways do you self-medicate? Your woundedness will heal only if you apply the proper medication; otherwise, the infection will just scab over. Stuffing or repressing keeps the pain alive, operating in the background of your life. It keeps you from healing as does stewing on past hurts, self-medicating with things, and attempting to maintain control. That pain will continue to operate in your life as long as you try to manage your woundedness.

Our alternative is to **go to God with our hurts**. Engage with Him about your pain. Be honest with Him about how you feel. You're not telling Him anything He doesn't already know. For us to heal, we must acknowledge what has happened and talk to God about it. As we do this, Scripture assures us that God cares about our pain, for "The LORD is near to the brokenhearted and saves the crushed in spirit."[3]

As we allow Him to examine our wounds, we will encounter sin we must confess and ways in which we must change. We will have to unlearn unhealthy coping mechanisms and cultivate new, God-honoring ways of responding, and as we identify lies we've believed, we'll need to replace them with truth. These are not things we can do on our own power, but as we spend time praying, studying, and meditating on God's Word, His Spirit will work in us, transforming us more and more into the image of Christ.

Not only can God sanctify us, He can make us whole. "He heals the brokenhearted and bandages their wounds,"[4] the psalmist tells us. While our past cannot be rewritten, it can be redeemed, and while our woundedness is something we will deal with throughout our time on this earth, there will be a day when we will be whole and renewed.

Our Enemy

What do you think of when you hear the words *spiritual warfare?*

Maybe you think about the cartoons where a person has an angel on one shoulder and a demon on the other with both trying to convince him to act a particular way. Maybe you've read *The Screwtape Letters* by C. S. Lewis, so you think of demons like Wormwood and Screwtape conversing about the best way to tempt you. When I was young (probably too young), I read Frank Peretti's fictional books *Piercing the Darkness* and *This Present Darkness*, and as a result, my imagination conjured up battles occurring between angels and demons in the spiritual realm that were akin to those in *The Lord of the Rings.*

But as Christians, we do not base our theology on cartoons or works of fiction. Our understanding of spiritual things should come from the Word of God, which states, "For our struggle is not against flesh and blood, but against the rulers, against the authorities, against the cosmic powers of this darkness, against evil, spiritual forces in the heavens."[5]

From the Bible, we learn that Satan and demons are real,[6] although they're not omnipresent, omniscient, or omnipotent. They're spiritual beings, but they're not God. They're created beings, not the Creator.

Furthermore, they cannot force us to sin. "The devil made me do it" is a fallacy, for the devil doesn't *make* us do anything. We act of our own volition. We don't need the devil's help to be tempted, for we are easily tempted by our own desires. While the devil and his demons can participate in our temptation, they are not directly tempting us each and every time.

At the same time, we do not need to underestimate the devil. First Peter 5:8 tells us that "the devil prowls around like a roaring lion, seeking someone to devour."[7] I wouldn't want to be in the vicinity of a ravenous lion looking for its next meal because lions don't show mercy to their prey. Similarly, the devil doesn't care about you. You reflect the image of God; therefore, he hates you and wants to destroy you because he hates the God you reflect. He'll exploit our weaknesses and our suffering as well as our victories—anything he can use to bring us down.

One of his biggest tools is deception. If we believe lies about ourselves, our situation, others, or God, then we'll easily give into sin. Behind every sin is a lie we have believed. If we believe our sin is worth the result, we do not fully understand the truth of sin being rebellion against the Creator and Judge of the universe.

Although she had physically ended the toxic relationship, a young woman I discipled—Jordan—would not emotionally let go of her ex. Over time, I observed a hard-heartedness in Jordan whenever I challenged her to delete her ex's phone number or unfollow her ex on social media. Jordan tried to justify her actions several different ways, but I soon identified a lie she believed: "I should be able to maintain contact with my ex in order to have an opportunity to learn boundaries and how to resist temptation."

Subtle, right? However, we should not put ourselves in situations where we'll be tempted. Scripture tells us to pray "lead us not into temptation"[8] and exhorts us to "flee" from sin (1 Cor. 6:18; 1 Tim. 6:11). We don't grow our ability to withstand temptation by exposing ourselves to more of it. Exposure therapy does not work when our problem is sin.

Instead, we should run from sin and pursue Christ. This is why Paul follows the command to flee sin with the charge to "pursue righteousness, godliness, faith, love, endurance, and gentleness" (1 Tim. 6:11). We fight sin by growing our love for God and by acting in obedience to God. But do you see how believing this lie was Jordan's way of justifying her actions? Satan attempts to deceive us in big and small ways, and we need to be alert to what we believe as well as what we desire.

As we talk about spiritual warfare, we must also remember the outcome. We do not fight a losing battle because God has already won the war. As Christians, we fight from a position of victory because of what Christ has accomplished. But so often, we fight against sin like we're unsure of whether or not victory is even possible.

Whether it's a battle in world history or an SEC football championship, one thing is true about each of these showdowns: neither side knew the outcome. The victory was up for grabs to whoever could out-strategize or out-last the other. But what if they had known the outcome *before* heading into battle? How would that have affected morale on both sides? How would both sides have acted if they'd known the outcome?

For us, that "what if" is actually a known reality! Our enemy, Satan, knows of his defeat, but he continues to fight. Why? It's not that he's stupid. It's because *we* do not act and live like we know of *his* defeat! As he continues to war against us, he's banking on our forgetfulness or ignorance of what God has done. He's the ultimate kamikaze trying to do as much damage as he can in the time he has left.

Rather than us fight sin from a position of uncertainty about our current battle—and here comes some good news at long last!—let us fight as though we're confident in the God *who has already won the war*. Want to know how?

Glad you asked. When Adam and Eve sinned in Genesis 3, sin entered the world, separating us from God. As long as we are on this earth, we will struggle with sin and experience its various effects. While our sinfulness, our wiring, our woundedness, and our enemy are categories that help us understand how sin has affected us and our world, they also demonstrate our need for restoration. Since we are unable to fix ourselves, we need Someone who can take what is broken and make it whole. We need Someone who can make *us* whole, and there's only one Person who fits that bill—Jesus Christ.

He exercised this power in Christ by raising
him from the dead and seating him at his
right hand in the heavens—far above every
ruler and authority, power and dominion,
and every title given, not only in this age but
also in the one to come. And he subjected
everything under his feet and appointed
him as head over everything for the church,
which is his body, the fullness of the one
who fills all things in every way.
Ephesians 1:20–23

≫ CHAPTER 4 ≪

The God Who Designed Us

AS MUCH AS I LOVE TO BROWSE THROUGH IKEA, I LOATHE HAVING to put together my purchased items. Even though I studiously read the directions, I always have a part or two left over, and my constructed item is never as sturdy as it should be. As you've probably gathered, I'm *not* mechanically inclined. Whenever I try to put something together, I can read the directions, but a disconnect exists when I try to do what they say.

Like IKEA furniture, God has a design for how His creation should work, but by our own actions, we choose whether to trust and adhere to His design. Genesis 1–2 explains how God created humanity, gender, sex, and marriage. As the Creator of the universe, God has the authority to tell us what to do. As our Designer, He knows what He made us for and the best way for us to live out His design. Furthermore, He loves His creation. He wants what is best for us, and His design reflects what is both best and loving.

Even in the perfection of Eden, God communicated boundaries to mankind when He instructed Adam not to eat the forbidden fruit. To eat the fruit would result in death, so God lovingly told Adam not to eat it. God says "no" because He knows what is best for us. We may not like it when God gives us boundaries or when God says "no" to things we want. We may even feel that He is harsh or unloving. But when God tells us "no," it's for our own good. He's being a good, loving parent.

What we believe about God, His authority, and His design shows itself in how we live and how we respond to the boundaries and commands He's provided in Scripture. Do we trust Him and His Word? Do we trust that our Creator knows what's best for His creation—with regard to our sexuality as well as every other area of life?

Is God Sexist?

God made us in His image, intentionally choosing for us to reflect Him and to represent Him as two genders. He could have chosen to create only one gender or more than two genders, but in His all-knowing wisdom, He made both men *and* women as His image-bearers. This gives dignity and value to both genders, for both are of equal value to God.

Our worth comes from who made us, whom we reflect, and what He says about us, which is that we are fearfully and wonderfully made (Ps. 139:13–14). We have value because of who we reflect, and men and women reflect Him in different ways.

As we study the Bible and consider God's value of people, we must read it through the lens of Genesis 1–2. God doesn't value one image bearer more than another. While the Bible records examples of the mistreatment of women, this does *not* mean that God values women less than men. It means that the Bible tells the truth—in uncomfortable detail—about what sinners do when they are out of step with God.

I recently finished studying Judges, and as the nation of Israel spiraled, doing what was right in their own eyes instead of God's eyes, the treatment of women degenerated. When God's people walk with Him, their treatment of others reflects it; they act with love, compassion, respect, and kindness toward one another (1 John 2:9–11). When people are far from God, their treatment of others reflects that too, as evidenced by sexism, racism, abuse, and oppression. God isn't sexist, but people can be. He values both genders as His image-bearers, but we often fail to do the same. Such failure points to our brokenness, not His design.

To examine God's value of women, we must look back at her creation in Genesis 2:

> Then the LORD God said, "It is not good for the man to be alone. I will make a helper corresponding to him." The LORD God formed out of the ground every wild animal and every bird of the sky, and brought each to the man to see what he would call it. And whatever the man called a living creature, that was its name. The man gave names to all the livestock, to the birds of the sky, and to every wild animal; but for the man no helper was found corresponding to him.[1]

After creating man, God makes the assertion that it's not good for man to be alone. Therefore, He would make him "a helper corresponding to him."[2] Even in the perfection of Eden, God deemed something as "not good."[3] Even in a perfect, sinless environment, Adam needed a helper because he could not fulfill God's plan alone. Looking back at the creation mandates in Genesis 1:28, the commands God gives to Adam and Eve require both genders, for one gender by itself cannot fully obey the commands to be fruitful, to multiply, to fill the earth, to subdue it, and to have dominion over all the animals. We cannot fulfill God's plan without mutual assistance.

I don't know how familiar you are with Alabama summers, but it gets unbearably hot and humid. In one recent summer, my air conditioning went out twice, and the only thing I could do to fix it was to pick up the phone and call an AC technician. Needing help does not mean I'm stupid or incompetent or inferior. It means that, while I am skilled in a few areas, I am not skilled in all areas, and praise the Lord, there *are* people who are skilled at fixing air conditioners!

In Genesis 2:18 when God says that He'll make Adam "a helper corresponding to him," the Hebrew word for this phrase is *ezer kenegdo*. *Ezer* means "helper," and lest you get your back up about a chauvinistic reading of this word, the Old Testament uses it sixteen times to refer to *God*. *He* helps *us*. *He* has what His people lack.

Like the person who fixed my air conditioning, a helper enables us to do something we cannot do on our own, so it is *not* a subordinate or demeaning term. In fact, a better translation of the word might be "necessary ally,"[4] for woman is not a supplement to man or a sidekick. She's needed. She's essential. She's indispensable because, without her, God's mission for humanity will not be completed. As God Himself asserted, her absence is "not good."

The word *kenegdo* explains what type of helper befits Adam's situation: "a helper corresponding to him." *Kenegdo* contains the idea of being corresponding to something while also being opposite or different from it. Physically, there are complementing differences between men and women, and we also have differences in how we approach relationships, how we process emotions, and how we think. In all of these ways, the two genders correspond to each other and are different from each other, and we need these differences. We are better together because of them!

God could have made Adam and Eve the same way, but He didn't. He chose to make them different ways out of different materials. Adam was molded like clay from dirt, and Eve was skillfully fashioned out of a rib. God also could have chosen to make them at the same time, but in His sovereignty, He didn't. He made the man first, then the woman. Why? This order of creation establishes *the man* as the firstborn, which in ancient cultures meant that the man ranks highest after his father and serves as the representative of all other family members. As a modern example, this "role of primogeniture" or the role and rights of being born first is how Prince William of Great Britain was identified as the next in line for the throne after his grandmother and father.

Adam was the firstborn of all creation, and even though Eve sinned first, God held Adam responsible for the whole human condition because the firstborn was responsible for the oversight of the family (Rom. 5:12, 19). In this creation order, we see God's design of male headship in the home. God made Adam, then Eve. God made the servant leader then the necessary ally. In this design, men and women remain equal in value but have different functions or roles, and it is only because of the Fall that men abdicate their responsibility or abuse their authority.

God's Design for Gender and Transgenderism

As we think about transgenderism, it subverts the idea that God has ordained our gender. Because a person does not feel like their birth-assigned gender is true for them, they desire to change it. Our sex and gender identity (our *perception* of whether we're male or female) matters because our birth-assigned gender is the way in which God chose us to reflect Him and represent Him. Whether or not we believe this does not alter it from being true. No matter what you believe about what causes gender dysphoria (confusion about gender identity), God sovereignly assigns a gender to each person.

Our authentic self isn't based on how we feel (for we all know how fickle our feelings can be) or the approval of others (which is also fickle). Whether or not we feel like the gender God has chosen for us, we as Christians must adhere to His design and choose to trust His truth about us. Our feelings— though important—do not alter how God created us. He is the Creator; we are the creation. As the creation, having the power to change our anatomy does not mean we have the authority to do so. As Andrew Walker asserts, "So this is why, ultimately, God has authority in the transgender debate. His voice deserves to be heard, and his opinion needs to carry ultimate weight. . . . This is a question of whether the Creator has the right to speak about his creation. And it is a question of whether a Creator has more knowledge of his creation than a small part of his creation."[5]

I want to acknowledge that many who struggle with gender dysphoria or transgenderism feel genuine pain because of the disparity between who they feel they are and what their birth-assigned gender is. For some, hearing themselves called by a name or pronoun that reflects their birth-assigned gender can stir up feelings of anxiety and thoughts of self-harm. I don't want to denigrate the suffering that some feel when they see themselves in a mirror or wear certain items of clothing that don't match their felt gender. While our true self is who God made us to be at birth, that doesn't mean it's always easy to live out. While not everyone reading this book experiences feelings of gender dysphoria, we've all felt dissatisfaction with who we are, especially when compared to who God created us to be. Let us, therefore, respond with compassion and care— as well as truth—to those who struggle with transgenderism or gender dysphoria.

God Created Us for Joy

Though God created us to know Him, we often stiff-arm Him because we don't trust that in His presence there is "abundant joy" and "eternal pleasures."[6] In other words, we don't think that knowing Him will pay off or be worth the cost. But here's the truth: God made us for joy, and that joy comes from knowing Him. We will not have joy when we are disconnected from the Source of it.

Instead of mining the depths of all He has to offer, we refuse to even give Him a chance. We settle for less than the pleasure God offers. When we do this, we demonstrate our ignorance about God and what He offers us.

Have you ever read Psalm 16? The author has clearly taken God up on joy. Notice that he says God's presence contains the "fullness of joy"—the most joy possible for humans to experience. How can the psalmist say this? Because this isn't just head knowledge for him. He's lived the reality of it, which enables him to later say in Psalm 19 that the Lord's ways rejoice the heart, are more desirable than gold, and are sweeter than honey (vv. 8–10).

At this point you may be thinking—*Okay. Sure, I know I should access this great joy that God offers. And the psalmist's words indicate that it's possible to feel it. But how did he get there? How did he come to experience this pleasure and joy?*

If we zoom out and look at this Psalm as a whole, we find the answer: the study of God's Word. *This* is what fuels the psalmist's enjoyment of the Lord. We don't have to wonder what God is like, for the Bible tells us.

In our relationships with people, we enjoy spending time conversing with the people we like, and like any relationship, our relationship with God grows when we speak *and* listen to each other. Speaking to God is what we do in prayer, and listening to Him is what we do when we read and study the Bible, which is God's message to us. Joy is a fruit of the Spirit (Gal. 5:22); and the more we spend time with God, the more He is cultivating spiritual fruit in our lives, including joy.

So, if ultimate pleasure and joy is found in God alone and access to that pleasure and joy is made possible by spending time with Him in prayer and the study of His Word, are you taking the initiative to engage in these things?

Knowing that God is the source of joy not only motivates us to engage in prayer and Bible study, it also empowers us to say "yes" to Him and "no" to sin. We can say no to the temporary because of the eternal. We can say no to instant gratification because we're playing the long game.

Do you struggle with consistency in studying God's Word on your own? It's often tempting to watch Netflix, hang out with friends, or sleep instead of spending time with God. You might *say* you want to know God, grow in your relationship with Him, and experience joy and satisfaction in Him. But when you look at how you spend your time, what do your choices indicate—that you're living for the temporary or the eternal? Consider the words of George Müller, an evangelist and orphanage director in the 1800s:

> I saw more clearly than ever, that the first and great primary business to which I ought to attend every day was, to have my soul happy in the Lord. The first thing to be concerned about was not, how much I might serve the Lord, how I might glorify the Lord; but how I might get my soul into a happy state, and how my inner man may be nourished . . . I saw that the most important thing I had to do was to give myself to the reading of the Word of God and to meditation on it.[7]

George Müller grasped the significance of Jesus' words in John 15:4: "Remain in me, and I in you. Just as a branch is unable to produce fruit by itself unless it remains on the vine, neither can you unless you remain in me."

Müller knew that the most important thing he could do was to abide in the True Vine, and he connected this to having his soul "happy in the Lord." God made us for joy, and joy only comes from knowing Him and being known by Him. This joy does not necessarily come easily, though. Day after day, we make the choice to spend time with God or not, and our choices reflect our functional belief system. Your choice reflects whether or not you truly believe that God created us for joy and that joy is found in Him. When you look at your life (both your sexual decisions and your life as a whole), does it show that you believe *God* is the Source of joy or that joy is elsewhere to be found?

God as Redeemer

"Our Lord and God, you are worthy to receive glory and honor and power, because you have created all things, and by your will they exist and were created. . . . You are worthy to take the scroll and to open its seals, because you were slaughtered, and you purchased people for God by your blood from every tribe and language and people and nation."
Revelation 4:11; 5:9

In the throne room scenes of Revelation 4–5, the worshipers highlight two reasons why the Lord deserves praise: He is Creator and Redeemer. He created and sustains all things, and when His creation was separated from Him because of sin, He did something about it. We were slaves to sin, but Jesus set us free, paying for our release with His own life.

Wonder how this relates to your sexuality? Notice in 1 Corinthians 6 how Jesus redeeming us from sin becomes the basis for Paul's instructions to flee sexual immorality:

> Flee sexual immorality! Every other sin a per-
> son commits is outside the body, but the per-
> son who is sexually immoral sins against his
> own body. Don't you know that your body is a
> temple of the Holy Spirit who is in you, whom
> you have from God? You are not your own, for
> you were bought at a price. So glorify God with
> your body.[8]

What is Paul saying? As a Christian, you belong to God—
and not just your soul, your body too. With His blood, Christ,
the spotless Lamb, bought our freedom. He was the ransom
paid for our release, satisfying God's wrath for sin. Although
we were enslaved to sin, now we who are Christians are set
free from our bondage to sin, Satan, and death (Rom. 6:11;
1 John 5:19; Heb. 2:15). As Paul explains in Colossians 1:13–14,
"He has rescued us from the domain of darkness and transferred us into the kingdom of the Son he loves. In him we have
redemption, the forgiveness of sins."

We can easily gloss over Paul saying we've been bought
with a price, but we need to understand the seriousness of
our sin and what it cost Christ. Do we truly get what He has
freed us from? We were "children of wrath" and "sons of disobedience" who deserved God's wrath and eternal judgment
but instead gained His pardon and adoption into His family
(Eph. 2:1–10).

But Jesus hasn't just freed us *from* sin's bondage and penalty; He has freed us *to* something as well. We are now free to
live for Him, and remembering His sacrifice motivates us to
praise Him and to pursue obedience to Him, right down to the
decisions we make about our sexuality.

Remembering the gospel—what we deserve for our sin
and what Christ has accomplished—motivates us. It's why it is
so important for us as Christians to tell "the old, old story, how
a Savior came from glory," and as the hymn reminds us: "O

victory in Jesus, My Savior, forever, He sought me and bought me with His redeeming blood; He loved me ere I knew Him, and all my love is due Him."[9] All my love is due Him because of what He's done.

So, when Paul tells us we've been bought with a price, we understand just how steep that price was. It cost Christ His life. *This* is why our bodies do not belong to us. *This* is why our lives do not belong to us. Jesus paid for us, body and soul.

We're totally willing to let Christ save us from the punishment of our sins. We *want* that. We're all about letting him save the "soul" part. But are you willing to trust Christ, not just as your Savior, but as the Lord over your sex life and your desires? Do you live as though your *body* is yours or the Lord's?

As Paul gives us commands regarding our sexual activity, not only does he remind us of our redemption, he reminds us that our "body is a temple of the Holy Spirit,"[10] which is another reason why we are not our own. This harkens back to the temple in the Old Testament. Back then, the temple in Jerusalem was where people went to worship God and to offer animal sacrifices for their sin. As Hebrews 9:11–12 explains, Christ is the sacrifice for our sins and the perfect high priest:

> But Christ has appeared as a high priest of the good things that have come. In the greater and more perfect tabernacle not made with hands (that is, not of this creation), he entered the most holy place once for all time, not by the blood of goats and calves, but by his own blood, having obtained eternal redemption.

We don't have to rely on animals anymore because Christ offered Himself as the perfect, ultimate sacrifice. This enables us to have an all-access pass to God. Because of His death and resurrection, we no longer have to go to the temple in Jerusalem to worship God, for the Spirit of God resides in us!

That's right, God still dwells in a temple, but *we* are now the temple! And as God required the temple in Jerusalem to be purified and void of anything that was considered unclean, He expects the same of us as the dwelling places of His Spirit. The holy, pure God of creation lives in us, and we must be dwellings that accurately reflect who resides in us.

Anytime we sin, we are choosing to go back to the slavery our Redeemer has already freed us from, and as Galatians 5:1 teaches, "For freedom, Christ set us free. Stand firm, then, and don't submit again to a yoke of slavery."

Remember, friend, Jesus didn't just pay for your soul. He paid for *all* of you—body and soul. Because of this and because He is your Maker, He has ultimate authority over you. Not only that, but His Spirit resides in you. Do you treat your body as though it's the place where God dwells? Do you believe God's ultimate design for humans is the right one? If not, why?

» CHAPTER 5 «

Why Sexual Sin Is Sin:
Sex Is Heterosexual

WHEN THE COLLEGE GIRLS I DISCIPLED BEGAN CONFESSING THEIR involvement in masturbation, we identified it as sin, but we couldn't verbalize *why* it is a sin. Some sexual sins—like adultery, prostitution, incest, bestiality, and homosexuality—are explicitly identified as sin in the Bible. But if you look up the word *masturbation* in your Bible's concordance, you're not going to find it—not even in *The Message*!

Thankfully, around this time our pastor started preaching a sermon series on 1 Corinthians, and when he got to 1 Corinthians 6, he preached what our church affectionately termed "the PG-13 sermons."[1] It was the first time in my life I'd ever heard a pastor say the word *masturbation* in a sermon, and in it, he answered the why question.

If my college girls and I knew God's design for sex, we would understand how certain acts do not align with His design and are, therefore, sin. In the sermon, our pastor listed characteristics of God's design for sex,[2] and while he used it to talk about pornography and masturbation, I have adapted and applied this framework to everything from oral sex to sexual fetishes when talking with girls.

"Is this sexual act permissible? Or is it sin?" If you've ever found yourself asking these questions, we're about to go there. For an action to be permissible, it must meet *each* of the characteristics of God's design for sex. A failure to line up on even one characteristic means that the act is contrary to God's design. So, let's look at what God's Word says about His design for sex.

God Created Us as Sexual Beings

> Therefore a man shall leave his father and
> his mother and hold fast to his wife, and they
> shall become one flesh. And the man and his
> wife were both naked and were not ashamed.
> Genesis 2:24–25[3]

In Genesis 2, God institutes marriage and commands the husband and wife to "hold fast" to each other and become "one flesh." Here, God sets the precedent of "leaving and cleaving." The notion of "holding fast" means that two distinct persons are glued or cemented together, and the "two becoming one flesh" clearly includes the sexual union, although it also has emotional and spiritual implications. Genesis 2 lets us know that God designed sex as a gift and provides parameters for how this gift is to be enjoyed—within the context of a heterosexual marriage.

God created us all—not just those who are having sex—as sexual beings. We have sexual desires because He designed us with a sex drive. Therefore, it is not a sin to desire marriage and to want to have sex. The question is whether or not we are submitting those desires to the lordship of Christ. Do we want the fulfillment of these desires more than we want to obey Christ?

Author Rosaria Butterfield notes, "Sexuality isn't about what we do in bed. Sexuality encompasses a whole range of needs, demands, and desires. Sexuality is more a symptom of our life's condition than a cause, more a consequence than an origin."[4] In light of this, a single person is just as much a sexual being as a married person; their difference lies in how they each respond to their sexual desires. Depending on the desire, the married person can act on it in the context of marriage while the single must abstain. They respond differently, but both singles and marrieds should obey Christ in how they express their sexuality.

The absence of sexual fulfillment does not mean that a single person is less of a human being. If that were the case, then Jesus was not fully human. Although a virgin, Jesus was also a sexual being. However, being a sexual creature is not synonymous with being sexually active.

Knowing not all of His creation would marry, God still chose to make men and women as sexual beings because their sexuality, among other things, points to deeper spiritual truths. In *Sex and the Supremacy of Christ*, John Piper states: "the *ultimate* reason (not the only one) why we are sexual is to make God more deeply knowable."[5]

Sexual intimacy is a temporary picture that points to eternal spiritual intimacy. What do I mean? When a man and woman enter the covenant of marriage (which we'll explore in greater detail later), they forsake all others. They're essentially saying to their spouse, "Only you get to know me this way. Only you get to know me this profoundly and this deeply." When we become a Christian, we enter a spiritual covenant with God and are expressing to Him, "Only you get to know me this way. Only you get to know me this profoundly and this deeply." Sex reveals a God who knows His people in the most profound of ways.

Now, I am *not* insinuating in any way that we have sex with God. Rather, sexual intercourse gives us a point of reference for how deeply God wants us to know Him. Sex between a husband and wife shows us a real-life parable for the relationship between Christ and the church. According to Ephesians 5, this earthly relationship pictures the gospel.

Even though I am single, having sexual desires also helps me and other singles to know God more deeply. How so? Because both marriage and singleness depict the gospel. As Sam Allberry observes, marriage demonstrates the shape of the gospel while singleness shows its sufficiency.[6] What does this mean? For singles, you enter into a covenant with Christ upon your conversion and are, in a sense, married. You become part of the bride of Christ, the church. While many singles would like the earthly reality of marriage, marriage is not a need because *you already have the deeper thing that marriage points to.* Your ultimate need is for Christ, not sex, a spouse, or marriage.

Both singles and married people can honor God with their sexuality. Sexual fidelity in marriage depicts the fidelity of Christ and His bride, and sexual holiness as a single testifies that Christ is our greatest source of satisfaction and fulfillment. If this is God's purpose for sex as it relates to marriage and singleness, we quickly see that sexual fulfillment is not a right or something that is promised to us. Neither is sexual fulfillment some sort of apex of the human experience. Earthly marriage is not ultimate, and neither is sexual fulfillment.

Sex Is Heterosexual

As a child of the '80s, I grew up in an era of teased bangs and crimped hair, and by the time I entered high school, homosexuality had begun hitting our TV screens in all sorts of TV shows. Since then, in lightning speed, homosexuality has gone from one or two references here and there to being all-out normalized. The same goes for its presence in politics. When it comes to marrying people of the same sex, this has gone from being banned to being legalized and celebrated.

In our current culture, the prevailing opinion is that people should be able to do what they want with their bodies and to love and marry whom they want. But is this assumption right? How should a Christian engage this sort of logic? Instead of asking ourselves, let's ask the Bible and see what God has to say.

Homosexuality is a greater issue than being able to love whomever we want. In Genesis 1–2, God could have created humanity and marriage to work any way He wished. He also could have created just one gender, but He didn't. Remember, one of the reasons He made humanity to begin with is to *reflect who He is*. As it turns out, He's so unfathomable that it takes at least two genders to help us have at least a basic understanding of who He is. God could have instituted marriage differently as well, but He chose for it to be between one man and one woman in a covenant relationship. As Kevin DeYoung states,

> The mystical union of Christ and the church—each "part" belonging to the other but neither interchangeable—cannot be pictured in marital union without the differentiation of male and female. If God wanted us to conclude that men and women were interchangeable in the marriage relationship, he not only gave us the wrong creation narrative; he gave us the wrong metanarrative.[7]

Homosexuality does not fit with Genesis 1–2, nor does it jive with the picture God intends marriage to represent (Eph. 5:22–33). With the one flesh union between a husband and wife, God intends for marriage to include both unity and diversity. There's diversity because it's two different genders, and there's a oneness, a unity, when the husband and wife come together in intercourse.

Gay sex lacks the diversity of heterosexual sex, and it does not allow for physical oneness in the same way as heterosexual sex. As Daniel Heimback states, "Sex is not for joining identical things, or just anything at all, or nothing at all. Unless sex brings corresponding differences together, it produces nothing of value, the parts never make up something whole, and sex never advances beyond individual isolation."[8]

While joined together, Christ and the church are also two different entities, and to adequately represent this relationship, earthly marriages must be between two distinct entities. Otherwise, the relationship would reflect two of the same: Christ with Christ or the church with the church. Therefore, to be an accurate picture of Christ's relationship with the church, we must have diversity and complementarity, a heterosexual relationship, not a homosexual one. In other words, gay unions don't tell the right story. They can't accurately depict the gospel, for one of the leading roles is missing. Only in a heterosexual union is the gospel story portrayed correctly.

What Both Testaments Say about Homosexuality

After bravely confessing her current struggle with same-sex attraction, Riley relayed her attraction to another girl and how she's frustrated with God for allowing her to have these desires in the first place. It's not like she wanted them or asked for them. So, as she is trying not to give into her desires, she's also wrestling with God about the fact that she has them.

Having walked alongside several girls who feel same-sex attracted, I can tell you that Riley is not alone in her struggle or her questions about God's sovereignty, character, or care for her. Culture would say that if our biology or psyche inclines us toward homosexuality, then we should follow whatever feels natural. However, we as Christians do not base our beliefs on culture or feelings, important as they are. We base our beliefs on Scripture, for the God who created gender, sex, and sexuality has more authority on the subject than any finite scientist, doctor, or therapist.

While psychology and biology can help us better understand ourselves and the world, they aren't the final authority on morality. God is. While culture constantly changes its stance on what's right and wrong, the Bible provides ultimate clarity. For example, when Leviticus 20:13 states that "If a man sleeps with a man as with a woman, they have both committed a detestable act," it's claiming that homosexual behavior is a sin. It does not make allowances for feelings or science.[9]

Furthermore, the Bible does not permit the "God made me this way" excuse for giving into our desires. As the Creator of the universe, God is the ultimate authority on biology and human sexuality. He knows every biological factor that could possibly contribute to a person's homosexual desire, and still, He declares homosexuality to be a sin.

Why would we *not* want homosexuality to be a sin? Could it be that we want the freedom to act on our desires? Or perhaps you have a loved one who is same-sex attracted and you want them to be able to act on their desires and experience love and sexual satisfaction. It can sting to realize our desires don't dictate what's true. A sexual act may be legalized or culturally lauded, but that doesn't make it right or acceptable to God.

When interpreting the Bible, one must always consider the context of the passage, the original audience, and the covenant under which the text falls. Leviticus is written under the

old covenant, and to understand what carries over to the new
covenant, we must examine what is affirmed, annulled, or augmented in the New Testament.

The New Testament affirms that homosexuality *is* a sin
(Rom. 1:21–28), but it does not contain any affirmation of capital punishment for homosexuality (which is not surprising
since God's people lived under the rule of the Roman Empire
instead of a theocracy and could not institute such laws).
However, 1 Corinthians 6:9 clearly states that "the unrighteous
will not inherit God's kingdom," and verse 9 identifies "males
who have sex with males" as unrighteous. To clarify, those
who repent of their sin *will* be admitted into God's kingdom,
but unrepentant, habitual sin should lead a person to question
whether or not they're a Christian.

Romans 1 highlights a progression of sin. People suppress
the truth about God that's shown in creation (vv. 18–20),
become futile in their thinking and darkened in their hearts
(v. 21), and worship idols (vv. 22–23). As a result, God "delivered them over in the desires of their hearts to sexual impurity, so that their bodies were degraded among themselves."[10]

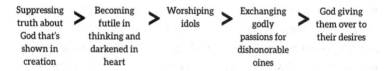

Suppressing truth about God that's shown in creation	>	Becoming futile in thinking and darkened in heart	>	Worshiping idols	>	Exchanging godly passions for dishonorable oines	>	God giving them over to their desires

Based on Romans 1, we see that sin distorts our thinking,
our desires, and our affections. Therefore, when it comes to
sexual desires or any other desire, we can't base our decisions on what we feel, want, or think is true. We must go back
to Scripture to determine truth. Our twisted or "unnatural"
desires indicate how sin has affected us (in this area as well
as others), not how God made us to be. As Jackie Hill Perry
asserts, "Desires exist because God gave them to us. But

WHY SEXUAL SIN IS SIN: SEX IS HETEROSEXUAL   59

homosexual desires exist because sin does."[11] Just because it feels good does not mean it is good for us. The goodness or rightness of an act is not based on feelings. Those change, but God's standards and design don't.

After exchanging truth about God for a lie and worship of Him for idolatry, Romans 1 shows how we exchange godly passions for dishonorable ones, specifically identifying homosexuality. Homosexuality goes against what nature clearly reveals about our anatomy and the complementary design of men and women's bodies. But suppression of God's truth means we cannot even read nature correctly. In other words, our entire view of reality is skewed because of the Fall.

As Paul wraps up a detailed list of sins in Romans 1, note his conclusion: "Although they know God's just sentence—that those who practice such things deserve to die—they not only do them, but even applaud others who practice them."[12] Because of our idolatry, God gives us up to our lusts and corrupted thinking (vv. 24, 28). This culminates not just in sinning ourselves *but in approving of the sin of others*, and approving of sin is a sin too. Christians who approve of homosexuality are approving of something God doesn't, which demonstrates how corrupted our thinking actually is.

So that's our first way of knowing whether or not a sexual act aligns with God's design—it must be *heterosexual*. We'll be discussing five more characteristics in the following chapters, and if you struggle with same-sex attraction (or any other sexual temptation), Part 3 is all about how to deal with sin and temptation. But for now, was there anything in this chapter that you question or disagree with? If so, note that in the reflection section provided, and specifically if you collide with something in this chapter, reflect on why that is. Even if you disagree with what you've read, I encourage you to continue reading through Part 2, for having the full biblical picture of

God's design for sex will provide further clarity and potentially answer any lingering questions.

Reflection Notes

_____

_____

_____

_____

_____

>> CHAPTER 6 <<

Why Sexual Sin Is Sin: Sex Is Relational

A FEW YEARS AGO, I TRAVELED TO THE MIDDLE EAST TO DO COM-munity development among Bedouin people. While teaching an English lesson to a room full of Bedouin women, one of the ladies next to me asked in broken English, "In America, man only have one wife?" I nodded yes, and she wistfully responded, "That's good. Much better."

Several of the women there were married to the same man, and the treatment of the wife and her children often depended on where she was in the pecking order. These particular wives were in competition with each other for their husband's favor and attention, and they were starved for affirmation, love, and hope. These women gave flesh and bones to the Old Testament stories I'd read about polygamy.

Polygamy never works well in the Bible, and that's because it goes against God's design. As seen in Genesis 1–2, God devised sex to involve two people, the husband and wife. He did not create multiple wives for Adam or multiple husbands for Eve. Genesis 2:24 points to marriage being monogamous: "This is why a man leaves his father and mother and bonds with his wife, and they become one flesh." At creation, monogamy—not polygamy—stands as God's template for marriage.

While sex is relational, God intends for it to occur in the context of the *marriage* relationship, which is a covenant between one man and one woman. So, as you've probably guessed by now, fornication and adultery are out. Polyamorous relationships ("loving" and having sex with more than one person) are out too, as is a married couple watching porn together to "fuel" their sex life since that's introducing a third-party into their relationship.

What about Masturbation?

When I was filling out an application to go back to school for counseling training, I had to temper my response when explaining why I was interested in the program. I wrote something along the lines of wanting to be better equipped to minister at my local church, but the blunt answer was masturbation. (Can you picture the eyebrows shooting up on the admission folks' faces if I'd written that?) Because so many of the girls I discipled struggled with this as well as other sexual sins, I recognized my need for more training, so I went back to school for a biblical counseling certificate.

As I continue to talk to girls about masturbation, I remain frustrated by the mixed messages Christians hear about masturbation (if they hear anything taught at all). I've encountered Christian authors and counselors who encourage masturbation, teaching that it's a benign method of sexual release for those who would pursue abstinence. Some therapists use masturbation as a way to help individuals coping with sexual trauma. Some say that the Bible doesn't give clear instructions on this topic and leave it up to individual conviction. However, we must go back to God's Word, for even when the Bible does not explicitly permit or prohibit an act, biblical principles help us determine whether something aligns with God's design.

Scripture portrays sex as a relational act between two people. In contrast, masturbation is solo sex. It serves the *self,* not someone else. Furthermore, because you do it to yourself, it is a homosexual act—a personal, homosexual act.[1] Even if you're thinking of the opposite gender in order to arouse yourself, you are stimulating yourself. *Your* gender doesn't change. In other words, it's a female (you) performing a sexual act on a female (also you). Therefore, masturbation violates God's design on the requirement of being heterosexual and relational. In a letter, C. S. Lewis noted additional concerns regarding masturbation:

> [Masturbation] . . . sends the man back into the prison of himself, there to keep a harem of imaginary brides. And this harem, once admitted, works against his *ever* getting out and really uniting with a real woman. For the harem is always accessible, always subservient, calls for no sacrifices or adjustments, and can be endowed with erotic and psychological attractions which no real woman can rival. Among those shadowy brides he is always adored, always the perfect lover: no demand is made on his unselfishness, no mortification ever imposed on his vanity. In the end, they become merely the medium through which he increasingly adores himself . . . [But] the *main* work of life is to *come out* of our selves, out of the little, dark prison we are all born in. Masturbation is to be avoided as *all* things are to be avoided which retard this process. The danger is that of coming to *love* the prison.[2]

But what if I'm thinking of my spouse while I'm masturbating? Or what if my spouse travels a lot for work or is deployed by the military? Or what if I'm now divorced or widowed—how do I deal with my pent-up sexuality? These are some of the questions I've been asked regarding masturbation.

With the business trip and deployment examples, being married doesn't change the fact that, when you're masturbating, you're stimulating yourself. Being married doesn't change masturbation being solo sex. God designed sex to be something a husband and wife do together, so even if you're thinking about your spouse to arouse yourself, masturbation is something you're doing to you. Therefore, it's homosexual, not heterosexual.

Furthermore, husbands and wives must be careful to nurture intimacy, and masturbation undermines that. With masturbation, it can become easier to rely on yourself for pleasure rather than to give of yourself to your spouse. Sexual desire should draw you together as a married couple, causing you to be dependent on each other for sexual fulfillment, but substituting masturbation for sex with your spouse damages your relationship by fostering sexual independence.

If you're divorced or widowed, I ache for you and the pain you've experienced. If you have been sexually traumatized, words cannot express the compassion and sorrow that I feel for you. Even though truth can often be hard to hear, it's because I care for you that I note that not even pain, loss, or victimization excuses masturbation. In the long run, it just makes things worse.

Whether you are single and never married or married and now single again, you are called to honor God with your body (1 Cor. 6:19–20). Being able to experience sex while married does not entitle you to masturbate when single again. The pent-up sexuality you feel is akin to what someone who's been sexually active and never married would feel if they were to repent and now follow God. We abstain from all forms of sexual immorality, which includes masturbation, and God gives grace to all to obey Him and withstand temptation.

Related to masturbation, I'm often asked about masturbation and having orgasms during sleep. One young woman I discipled had been sexually active and masturbated prior to becoming a Christian, and in her early days of following Christ, the urge to masturbate was strong. One day, she came to me so upset and worried because at night she would dream of having sex and masturbating and would wake up, feeling like she had masturbated in her sleep. She felt doubly guilty—for what she had dreamed *and* done in her sleep.

While we can control our influences—what we think about, watch, or read—before going to sleep, we can't control our dreams or what our bodies do when we're asleep. Whether awake or asleep, masturbating is still a personal homosexual act and, therefore, a sin whether we are awake or asleep when we do it. But there is grace for this just like there is grace for any other sin that you bring to Christ in repentance. You can't change what happened, and other than praying and being cautious with your influences, you can't really do much to prevent masturbating while asleep. But you can confess it to God and rest in His forgiveness and grace if it happens. As Romans 8:1 reminds us, "Therefore, there is now no condemnation for those in Christ Jesus." He has paid for our sexual sins in full—both the conscious and unconscious ones.

What about Sexual Fantasy and Erotica?

As weird as it may sound, her confession was my favorite type to hear.

I've heard many women confess sin over the years, and there are different types of confessions. There's "Sorry Not Sorry Samantha" who's either sorry she's been caught or sorry for the consequences—but not actually sorry for her sin. There's "Guilty Gabriella" who feels guilty over her sin but isn't willing to stop doing it. There's "Crying Clara" who cries over her sin, wants to change, and is actually willing to change but who lacks follow-through in doing anything to change. There's "Wrestling Wren" who is struggling because the Bible doesn't jive with how she feels or wants to live, and she's sorting out whether to side with God or her flesh. Then there's "Repentant Ramona" who feels contrition over her sin, wants to change, and is taking steps to turn from sin.

She was a Repentant Ramona. Convicted of her sin, she confessed it to a friend and to me, and the confession was two-fold: masturbation and sexual fantasies.

With sexual fantasies, I'm not referring to sexualized night-mares or flashbacks as a result of trauma, and if night terrors or flashbacks are something you experience, please talk to a counselor or a mature Christian of the same gender about this and allow them to help you work through your trauma.

With sexual fantasies, there's a difference here for single women and married women. Married people are free to sexu-ally daydream *about their spouse*, but sexual fantasies become a sin when they're about anything or anyone other than their spouse or when they're visualizing something dishonoring, degrading, or harmful toward their spouse. Since single people do not have a spouse, there is no one they can think about sexually without it being lustful and sinful.

Another note for those who are married: as you fantasize about your spouse, are you imagining your spouse as he is, or are you imagining him as you want him to be, pandering to your every whim or lacking the idiosyncrasies that quit being cute years ago? Are you playing God with your spouse, con-trolling or manipulating him in your mind? Even in our imagi-nation, we must be careful not to objectify someone (even our spouse) or to worship the idol of control!

What fuels our sexual fantasies? For Repentant Ramona, she used sexual daydreams to cope with feeling unwanted and with desiring someone to want her. For others, sexual fantasies are a means to masturbation. One college student mentioned how she rationalized her sexual fantasies by telling herself that she needed to visualize and think through what to do when having sex to prepare herself for the day when she would, Lord-willing, get married. Another girl relayed that she would indulge in homosexual plot lines in her mind since she knew she couldn't act on them in real life. In other words, she attempted to maintain physical purity by engaging in mental impurity, which is an example of how we rationalize our sin.

Motivations vary from person to person, but ultimately, we give into sexual fantasies because of our selfish desires. During the Sermon on the Mount, Jesus expands our understanding of adultery to encompass lust, which happens in our minds and affections. He builds upon the seventh commandment when He states, "You have heard that it was said, 'Do not commit adultery.' But I tell you, everyone who looks at a woman lustfully has already committed adultery with her in his heart."[3]

Jesus' teaching specifically addresses the sin of lusting after another man's wife. The Greek word for *lustfully* (*epithymesai*) means "to have a sexual interest in someone, desire."[4] Lust occurs when we objectify and sexually think about someone who is not our spouse, and in this text, Jesus equates desire with deed. Lusting after someone is tantamount to acting out sexually with them. Even if the figures of our imagination aren't real people, it's still sin.

Not only are sexual fantasies an expression of lust, they're also perversions of truth. In them, we create a world in our minds where *we* rule, not God. In these fictional fantasies, life happens as we want it, not as God wills it. We do what is right in our own eyes without consideration of God and what He deems right and holy. We act as though it's our world and our rules. But it's not. God's authority extends to our imagination.

In Matthew 5, Jesus raises the standard of the seventh commandment and relates it to the tenth commandment, which is about coveting. Some might argue that sexual fantasies don't hurt anyone since the activity is contained to the mind, but Jesus' teaching indicates that lustful thoughts *do* affect others. They affect you *and* the person you've objectified. Lust is not a private affair. While the other person may not know how you have dehumanized them by mentally playing out your self-indulgent fantasies, you blatantly disobey the command to love your neighbor as yourself when you do this.

In the Sermon on the Mount, Jesus distinguishes between external and internal righteousness. The Jewish religious leaders (like many people today) thought that they were innocent as long as they avoided external sins such as murder, lying, cheating, etc. In contrast, Jesus demonstrates how the internal part of us is also unclean. You may not murder someone, but internally, your anger, jealousy, and resentment toward others is just as sinful (Matt. 5:21–26). You may not have had sex with someone outside of marriage, but if you think lustful thoughts about another, it's just as bad (Matt. 5:27–30). Jesus elevates the importance of what we do with our thoughts and emotions. He requires internal *and* external righteousness, and we're not capable of either on our own. It's why we need Him to work in us!

I would be remiss in tackling the subject of fantasy if I did not address erotica, for it is fantasy in book form. It capitalizes on emotion, emphasizing the relationship and the deep connection between the people who are "in love." We read erotica for the same reasons we fantasize—because we feel dissatisfaction, we want to escape reality, we desire affirmation, we want to be aroused, we're looking for ideas of how to spice up our sex lives, etc. Reading sex scenes in books does not align with the Bible's definition of righteousness, no matter why you're doing it. It's a sin to watch someone have sex on a screen, and it's a sin to read about it.

In Song of Solomon 2:7, Solomon's bride urges the young women of Jerusalem not to "stir up or awaken love until the appropriate time." Erotica intends to arouse, yet a practical application of Song of Solomon 2:7 is not to arouse ourselves "until the appropriate time." If you're single, you're not to arouse yourself or awaken love until you're married. If married, your spouse should be who arouses you, not what you read on a page or watch on a screen.

Fantasy and erotica turn us inward, taking us deeper within ourselves and causing us to waste time on what isn't reality. By spending time with the imaginary people in our minds, we miss out on real relationships with real people. By looking inward with fantasy, we miss out on the life God has for us, selfishly squandering the time He's given to us.

In *Knowing God*, J. I. Packer states, "For love awakens love in return; and love, once awakened, desires to give pleasure."[5] When I think about God's love for me and how He sent Jesus to die on a cross in order to give me the opportunity to have a relationship with Him, how can I not be overwhelmed by His love? Remembering His love stirs in me a desire to please Him. I want to demonstrate my gratitude and affection by showing Him love, and as Jesus clearly explains, "The one who has my commands and keeps them is the one who loves me."[6]

In Matthew 22:37, Jesus calls us to love Him with all of our *mind*. We're to love Him with how we think about Him, ourselves, others, and things, for our obedience to God involves thinking pure thoughts (Phil. 4:8). With this, do you live as though God knows your thoughts? Do you live as though He cares about the content of your daydreams? Are you attempting to love God with *all of your mind*?

What about Bestiality?

You may question whether people actually struggle with bestiality, but the Bible talks about it. Also, sexual union with animals is moving faster and closer to our cultural horizon than we may think, so it's important to note that God's design for sex is species-specific. Humans—not animals—are made in God's image, so while we're to respect and care for animals as part of God's creation, animals are not on an equal playing field with humans.

Furthermore, a female dog cannot complement a male human, for example, even if it is a "heterosexual" relationship. As Daniel Heimbach explains, "It may involve partners who are sexually *different*, but they do not *correspond*. No animal can ever *complement* the sexual nature of any human partner no matter what gender it happens to be."[7]

God explicitly prohibits bestiality in Leviticus 18:23:[8] "You are not to have sexual intercourse with any animal, defiling yourself with it; a woman is not to present herself to an animal to mate with it; it is a perversion." Bestiality deviates from His design, and in verse 24, God continues to explain *why* He prohibits His people from defiling themselves via bestiality: ". . . for the nations I am driving out before you have defiled themselves by all these things." The Canaanites defiled themselves by practicing such vulgarity. As a result, God punished them, and He warns His people against making the same sinful choices and reaping similar consequences.

With Leviticus and Old Testament Law, one can discern God's design by looking at what He blesses and what He disciplines. The consequence He gives for bestiality is the death penalty for both the person and the animal (Lev. 20:15–16), and this gives us a baseline for understanding how seriously God takes this particular sin. U.S. laws do not currently permit capital punishment for bestiality, and because Scripture tells us to "submit to the governing authorities,"[9] we do not pursue vigilante justice for this or other sins such as adultery, homosexuality, or incest. My point is simply that God takes bestiality seriously, and so should we.

Why spend time discussing bestiality? Because if culture dictates that "I can love and be loved by whoever I want and that I can do what I want with my body," eventually it will ask the question, "Why can't I love and be loved by my cat or dog? After all, love is love." Bestiality could potentially be appealing because animals won't reject or emotionally hurt you like humans do. Furthermore, when thinking about the rise of emotional support animals, couldn't an unhealthy emotional attachment lead to acting out sexually with them (much as it can with codependent human relationships)?

As Dr. Allen Ross asserts, ". . . although the moral impurity of this world is perverse and detestable by any simple assessment, the more it is tolerated the more acceptable and appealing it becomes."[10] Bestiality needs to be on our radar of things we talk about and teach on as Christians. Nothing is new under the sun, and since God has explicit commands about bestiality in Scripture, we don't need to be naïve enough to think it's not also happening today.

What about Sexbots, Sex Toys, and Sexual Fetishes?

In the fall of 2018, attempts were made to open the first U.S. robot brothel in Houston, Texas,[11] and there's already "love doll brothels" in Canada, Spain, Italy, and Russia. The concept is that of any other brothel except that, instead of a person, human-like dolls can be rented or purchased and used in private rooms at the brothel.

These sexbots have humanoid skeletons and a synthetic skin covering, and some can even talk dirty, moan, and sigh when touched. They may look like humans, and they may even sound and respond like humans. But they remain machines, lacking a human soul, and a non-human cannot amply substitute for an image-bearer of God. Intimacy with a machine is not a suitable substitute for human intimacy.

While arguments are made that robot brothels curb STD transmission and directly lead to the decrease of human sex slaves, we must not forget God's design and the sinfulness of man. Sex being relational has implications for the use of sex robots, sex dolls, and sex toys. In Genesis 1:28, God commands Adam and Eve: "'Be fruitful, multiply, fill the earth, and subdue it.'" But we cannot be fruitful if we act out sexually with non-humans.

God only permits sex to occur between *people*, more specifically, between a husband and wife. Therefore, sexual acts with a doll or robot are against His design. Furthermore, the novelty of a doll will wear off, and other novelties will be sought to give the person the same sexual satisfaction. Sin isn't satisfied for long. Engaging in sin will only provide momentary gratification; then, the emptiness will inevitably return.

Sexbots and sex dolls are only two types of sex toys. Broadly speaking, sex toys are any items or devices used to stimulate or enhance sexual pleasure, so sex toys range from vibrators to feathers to blindfolds to handcuffs. Based on God's design for sex, the use of such things in sexual acts outside of marriage is a sin, but what about within the marriage relationship? Can a husband and wife use sex toys together to the glory of God?

Since sex toys are not specifically referenced in Scripture, we must consider several questions to determine if biblical principles permit the use of sex toys within marriage. These questions are especially important to note since various sex toys are used in BDSM (bondage, dominance, sadism, and masochism) practices.

- Does it inflict harm?
- Is its use respectful and loving?

- Is its use consensual?
- Is its use selfless or selfish?
- Is its use beneficial to the marriage relationship, both in the short-term and in the
  long run?
- Does its use hinder trust in the marital
  relationship?
- Are you more interested in the toy than
  your spouse?
- Are you dependent or even addicted to its
  use, so that you can't have sex without it?

In discussing sexbots and sex toys, sexual fetishes also require a mention. According to the DSM-V, people who have a fetishistic disorder experience sexual arousal from objects or parts of the body that are not typically regarded as erotic. Also, the fetish typically has a multisensory aspect to it—holding, wearing, rubbing, smelling, or tasting the object. To be diagnosed a disorder, the fetish must occur for at least six months, involve the use of nonliving things, cause distress or impairment in various aspects of life (socially, vocationally, etc.), and the objects are not limited to clothes used in cross-dressing or devices such as a vibrator that are used for genital stimulation.[12]

"How do you end things with a guy who tells you he has a sexual fetish with teacups, diapers, wigs, and dresses?" asked the girl sitting across the table from me. Dating is a process of evaluating whether or not the other person is someone you can and should marry, so when this young woman told me that a guy she'd dated revealed this about himself, we agreed—this red flag warranted a swift end to the relationship!

Engaging in sexual fetishes is sin because a person acts out sexually with some*thing* rather than someone. It's akin to besti-ality but with an object instead of an animal. When the person with the fetish prefers to have a sexual partner wear or utilize the fetish object, it is still a sin because the sexual stimulation is still about an object, not a person; there just happens to be another person involved. When some*thing* is required or strongly preferred for sexual excitement, it's a problem. More than that, it's a deviation from God's design for sex.

Having the label of a clinical disorder does not change the fact that acting on a fetish either mentally or physically is a sin. A person's biology may cause suffering and create challenges for them, but our biology does not make us sin. We either choose to obey God or our desires.

Because mainstream culture currently views fetishes as deviant behavior, people who struggle with fetishism will likely hide it until they can't. The guilt and shame accompanying this struggle is compounded if the person is a Christian. If you are reading this and fetishism has been or currently is part of your life, know that (1) it's not just you and (2) God calls us to turn away from sin and trust in Him. He knows, He cares, and He is with you in this struggle. Furthermore, even though it won't be easy to resist, He does give us the strength necessary to withstand sinful urges. He offers grace for our sin and promises to forgive us if we confess our sins to Him (1 John 1:9). Fetishism is not beyond the power of His grace and mercy, and if you do struggle in this way, I urge you to seek professional help.

If you are reading this as a church leader or disciple-maker, be cognizant of the possibility that believers you know might struggle with this particular sin. While you may not understand it, do not treat it as an unforgivable sin because it isn't. If someone comes to you and admits this is a struggle, treat them with dignity and compassion just as Jesus treated the sinners He encountered. Treat them the way you would want to be treated if you had the courage to let another person in on your variety of sinfulness.

What about BDSM?

The most awkward conversation I've ever had with my boss (one of our church's pastors) occurred when he proofread a women's ministry blog post I wrote on BDSM back when the first *50 Shades of Grey* movie released. While BDSM (bondage, dominance, sadism, and masochism) has been around long before the *50 Shades* books and movies, the trilogy definitely made it famous.

Everything that I previously wrote about sex toys applies to BDSM. However, BDSM deserves its own section because of the relational implications of its practices and because we should differentiate between BDSM and sexual play that is healthy and appropriate between a husband and wife.

What is BDSM exactly? It's not just kinky sex. *Sadism* involves a "dominant" who enjoys inflicting pain on another person, "the submissive," and this often involves the use of physical objects as well as verbal abuse. A *masochist* is one who enjoys, on some level, receiving pain and humiliation.

While sadism and masochism have to do with intentionally inflicting and receiving pain as a means of sexual or psychological pleasure, *bondage* and *dominance* are the means of doing so. The dominant binds and mistreats the submissive with the intent of arousing one or both of them. The submissive agrees to such treatment, which is often where a contract comes in, and as Gary Thomas writes, "Let's be honest. If your lover leads you to a place that looks like the 'Spanish Inquisition,' you're in a horror movie, not a romance."[13]

While BDSM is relational in the sense that it occurs between two people, it does *not* line up with the Bible's standard for how a relationship should function. BDSM fits the category of abuse, not love, and *abuse has no place* in sex or in marriage. First Corinthians 13 defines love as kind, not insisting on its own way, and not rude. These ideas do not describe BDSM.

Could you accurately substitute BDSM for love in 1 Corinthians 13:4–6?

> BDSM is patient and kind; BDSM does not envy or boast; BDSM is not arrogant or rude. BDSM does not insist on its own way; BDSM is not irritable or resentful; BDSM does not rejoice at wrongdoing, but rejoices with the truth.[14]

It doesn't work, does it? BDSM—sexual violence—destroys intimacy and trust between partners, and it distorts the biblical understanding of what headship and submission should look like in marriage, which is how God designed the relationship between the husband and wife to function.

Ephesians 5 presents us with a biblical picture for how this relationship should function. It does portray the husband as the "head" of the wife, but look at what verse 25 says about *how* he's to lead: "Husbands, love your wives, just as Christ loved the church and gave himself for her."

The husband is told to follow the pattern of Christ in how he loves and treats his wife, and Christ's pattern lacks any hint of abusing power. A husband's authority does not mean he can do whatever he pleases; instead of seeking to be served, a husband should seek to serve his wife as Christ sacrificially serves His Bride, the church. Does any of this sound like "the dominant" partner in BDSM? Absolutely not! Jesus didn't come to harm or assault people; He came to save them. Biblical authority looks like laying down your life so that the other can flourish.

Ephesians 5:22–24 also depicts the wife as submitting to her husband. To clarify, submission does not mean that one must 100 percent agree or that they cannot voice their opinions. Nor does it mean a person should follow someone into sin, for we should submit to Christ first and foremost. We have a mind of our own, an identity of our own, and a relationship with Christ on our own. Submission does not negate any of this. A wife is not less-than just because she has a different role. Husbands and wives stand equal before God. They are both image-bearers of God and co-heirs with Christ, and one is not worth more than the other.

Grasping the symbolism of Ephesians 5 helps us understand submission. Wifely submission to one's husband reflects the church's submission to Christ, and a husband's love for his wife reflects Christ's love for the church. Furthermore, *both* husbands and wives ultimately submit to Christ. This looks nothing like "the submissive" in BDSM, for that person passively goes along with the dominant partner who leads them both into sin and harm. For a woman to become the submissive in a BDSM relationship demonstrates, at the very least, an ignorance of biblical submission.

With BDSM, it's important to note that it's not always men who take the dominant roles and women who take the submissive roles. But no matter the role you have taken or fantasize taking, the biblical pattern we're called to remains unchanged. Furthermore, Jesus remains our model for how to treat one another, and He doesn't treat people in harmful or degrading ways.

If you're engaging in BDSM, have you considered that God loves you and does not want you to be harmed but honored? He doesn't want you to be humiliated or assaulted—neither does He want you to do such things to others. True intimacy with God does not come from Him hurting or assaulting us but from Him serving, loving, and cherishing us. If that's true of our intimacy with God, why would our intimacy with others look any different? If you struggle in this way, have you ever considered that needing these things in order to achieve intimacy or pleasure tells the wrong story about the way God is intimate with us?

Ultimately, BDSM serves as a counterfeit, a substitute for wanting a man to act like a man, to take charge, and to initiate, and for the masochist in the relationship, it demonstrates a twisted passivity that requires pain to get sexually excited or to feel loved. It normalizes abuse with one person having power and control while the other person consents to the abuse. In light of all of this, engaging in BDSM within the context of marriage mocks the picture of Christ's eternal marriage with His people.

You might be wondering, if you are married, if any sort of sexual play is allowed *at all.* Are things like blindfolds—or closing your eyes in order to pay attention to other senses— totally off the table? What's the difference between sexual play and BDSM? This goes back to the question about the ethics of sex toys in marriage. Do both partners feel loved and safe? Is it humiliating, demeaning, abusive, or disrespectful to one or both people? Is the use of such items selfish or selfless? Does the use of an item cause one or both spouses to relive past trauma or abuse? How does this affect the marriage relationship in the short-term and long-term? Does its use build trust or erode trust? Does the use of this item cultivate a dependency where sexual excitement cannot occur without it? While BDSM differs from sexual play, as Dannah Gresh notes in *Pulling Back the Shades*, "Sexual play, even within marriage, crosses the line if it ever causes physical harm, is degrading, or violates your will."[15]

God is not anti-pleasure. He is the One who created sex in the first place! So if it does not go against His design and His Word, if does not cause harm or have mastery over you, and if it fosters love and true intimacy in your marriage, then go for it! God wants you to enjoy having sex with your spouse, but the Enemy wants to deceive you and make you feel as though you are missing out.

If you are single, he might be trying to convince you that you're missing out by not being married and having sex. If you are married, the lie might be that BDSM could spice up your sex life and that you're missing out if you don't at least try it. In both cases, the enemy's intent is to get you to move outside of God's good design, just like he did with the very first couple on the planet (Gen. 3:5–6). Don't listen to him.

Whether single or married, God is the ultimate source of pleasure. On top of that, He gives you things to enjoy in this life that are within His design—things He's given you full permission to explore. Put your eyes on those things instead of the things that are outside of His will for you. Or, as Dr. Juli Slattery puts it, "God is the greatest proponent of your pleasure—not the pleasure that is sweet for a season, but the deep, profound satisfaction that only grows sweeter with time. Once you understand what God has said 'no' to, you are free to have a great time exploring all he has given you to enjoy."[16]

>> **CHAPTER 7** <<

Why Sexual Sin Is Sin: Sex Is Covenantal

THE CULT CLASSIC *THE PRINCESS BRIDE* IS ONE OF MY FAVORITE movies, and as the clergyman famously proclaims at the wedding of Buttercup and Prince Humperdinck: "Mawage. Mawage is what bwings us together today. Mawage, that bwessed awangement—that dweam within a dweam . . ."[1] While God created sex to be heterosexual and relational, He also designed it to exclusively occur in the "bwessed awangement" of "mawage," a covenant relationship between a husband and wife.

God sovereignly chose to bookend the Bible with marriage. Genesis 2 tells of the first marriage, and Revelation 19 describes the coming marriage supper of the Lamb. The storyline of the Bible includes mention of various covenants God has made with His people, and it culminates with a new covenant that is made between God and those who trust in Him for salvation. Working with a singles ministry, I see many people who want to enter a marriage covenant but who do not grasp the place they already have in a covenant with Christ! Understanding this greater covenant we're part of as Christians informs the other covenants we enter into—such as marriage. In short, our earthly family units are to be patterned after the family of God, not the other way around.

In thinking about various covenants in the Old Testament, God gave a rainbow as a sign of His covenant with Noah (Gen. 9:11–17), and it reminded humanity of His promise to never again destroy the world with a flood. In His covenant with Abraham, God designated circumcision as the covenant sign that He'd make Abraham's descendants as numerous as the sand on the seashore, give his descendants the land of Canaan, and bring kings from his line (Gen. 15; 17). An important observation about God's covenant with Abraham: God alone makes this promise. It's not tit for tat, where you do this and I'll do that. God's promises were unilateral and without conditions. God also doesn't need covenants or signs of covenants; He doesn't need anything. He's provided them for our sake, to demonstrate His commitment to His promises even though we're often unfaithful to ours.

In His covenant with Israel at Mt. Sinai, God expanded on the covenant with Abraham, naming Israel as His people and calling them to observe the signs of His covenant with them— circumcision and Sabbath (Exod. 31:12–17). While God would keep His promises, the people's observance of circumcision and Sabbath reminded them of their obligations as covenant members.

In the new covenant, we have the signs of baptism and the Lord's Supper. These stand as visible reminders of promises made. They're important because promises are invisible. They're not tangible. But the signs of the covenant are visible and tangible.

In the marriage covenant, sex is the sign. The physical act of becoming one flesh constitutes the sign of the covenant made between a husband and wife before God. Therefore, sexual intercourse is not necessarily the reward for getting married. As John Piper states, "That would be like saying baptism is the reward we receive for becoming a Christian. No, sex is the sign of the marriage covenant itself. And to engage in sex is to call God as witness to hold us accountable for covenantal commitment."[2]

When we love someone, we want to express that love and make promises to that person. The marriage covenant creates a space where those promises have more meaning because you legally bind yourself to another. As Timothy Keller describes in his book *The Meaning of Marriage*: "Someone who says, 'I love you, but we don't need to be married' may be saying, 'I don't love you enough to curtail my freedom for you.' The willingness to enter a binding covenant, far from stifling love, is a way of enhancing, even supercharging it."[3]

A marriage covenant is more than just a contract or agreement between two people for the benefit of individual satisfaction and fulfillment. If we view marriage as merely a contract, then it's something we enter into for our own benefit, and as soon as it's not beneficial to us, we break the contract. For many people, a lack of self-actualization or a lack of satisfaction in marriage constitutes a good enough reason for divorce, and such consumeristic views value the desires of an individual more than the covenantal commitment made to God and to the spouse. But this view of marriage is *not* God's view.

What about Divorce and Remarriage?

In the most unique wedding ceremony I've attended, the bride delivered a heartfelt set of vows that she wrote, and she went first, which is unusual since traditionally the groom says his vows first. But then the officiant turned to the groom, who is a computer programmer, and asked, "Command C, command V?" (For those of you not up on your computer lingo, this means "copy and paste.") The audience chuckled, and if you knew the couple, their quirky choice of wedding vows would not be a surprise.

In traditional wedding vows, a minister will pronounce the couple as husband and wife and state: "Those whom God has joined together let no one put asunder."[4] The liturgy reminds us that *God* joins together a husband and wife and that we should not unmake what He has made. In Matthew 19, a question about the lawfulness of divorce prompts Jesus' teaching on the subject, and in His response, Jesus points us back to God's creation design in Genesis 1–2, a subtle reminder that just because something is lawful does *not* mean that it's moral or righteous to God.

In Scripture, God provides two clear, biblical reasons for divorce: sexual immorality (Matt. 19:9) and when an unbeliever wants to divorce their Christian spouse (1 Cor. 7:10–16). Even in these situations, Scripture does *not* teach that one *has* to get a divorce; it simply expresses that divorce is permissible in these situations. Divorce is not God's best, but it's also not a sin *if it's for a biblical reason* (e.g., sexual immorality or abandonment by an unbelieving spouse). However, reasons such as unhappiness, falling out of love, losing touch with who you are, unmet expectations, incompatibility, and a lack of intimacy do *not* constitute biblical reasons for divorce.

Questions often arise about whether abuse or neglect by one's spouse qualifies as biblical reasons for divorce. While the Bible does not provide explicit teaching on this, an abused spouse is being sinned against and should immediately take action to be safe. In such circumstances, separation is often necessary in order to ensure safety. An abused spouse should *not* stick around to experience further mistreatment.

While theologians differ on whether abuse is a biblical reason for divorce, Wayne Grudem argues for this based on a phrase in 1 Corinthians 7:15: "But if the unbeliever leaves, let him leave. A brother or a sister is not bound in such cases. God has called you to live in peace."

While Paul specifically addresses desertion by an unbelieving spouse in 1 Corinthians 7, the phrase "in such cases" references that there are situations that could release someone from the marriage covenant other than the original situation presented in this text. Grudem contends that abuse in marriage should be included as part of "such cases" because the abuser has destroyed the marriage covenant with their actions, causing harm in more ways than desertion ever does.[5]

When is remarriage permissible for someone who has been divorced? Scripture gives two scenarios in which remarriage is biblical:

1. The offended spouse in cases of adultery
   (Matt. 19:1–12; Mark 10:1–12)
2. The Christian spouse who is abandoned by
   their unbelieving spouse (1 Cor. 7:10–16)

To be clear, a person who commits adultery and whose spouse divorces them because of the adultery is *not* permitted to remarry. They are the *offending* party in the matter, breaking the marriage covenant with their adultery. While the offending spouse cannot remarry, the *offended* spouse can. It is comparable to how a person can remarry after the death of their spouse.

With regard to 1 Corinthians 7, disagreement exists over whether Christians who have been abandoned and divorced by their unbelieving spouse can remarry, and the dispute has to do with how one interprets verse 15: "But if the unbeliever leaves, let him leave. A brother or a sister is not bound in such cases. God has called you to live in peace."[6]

No matter the interpretive stance regarding remarriage, divorce should never be flippantly pursued. A Christian spouse should genuinely seek to save the marriage. But if the unbelieving spouse is unwilling to reconcile, the divorced Christian spouse has not sinned, and we should not treat them as though they have.

Some who read this might recognize that they have sinned—either knowingly or unknowingly—in getting divorced or remarried. Thankfully, we serve a God of grace and mercy. If you haven't already, confess your sin to Him and ask for His forgiveness. Divorce and remarriage are not unforgivable sins, and while we cannot change our past, God can forgive it and redeem it.

Keep in mind, though, that God's grace is never an excuse to sin (Rom. 2:4). Yes, He will forgive those who repent, but you miss the point of the gospel if you think it's okay to divorce or to remarry under unbiblical circumstances because God will forgive you later.

If you do *not* have biblical grounds for divorce (and are not in a situation where you need to separate for safety's sake), how can you get help for your marriage? This might involve counselors, pastors, small group leaders, mentors, etc. What are the areas of conflict? How can they be addressed? What do you need to do? You cannot control your spouse, but you can choose to work on yourself. You can choose to respond to conflict in a Christlike manner. You can intentionally seek ways to serve your spouse and to demonstrate love to them, even if they don't deserve it. None of these things are easy, but as you pursue Christ, His Spirit will change *you* from the inside out and give you the strength to obey Him.

What Do We Do with Our Sexuality If We're Single?

Have you ever participated in a conversation with someone who was so angry you could feel the heat radiating from them? Sitting across from me at a restaurant was a young woman, and intertwined in her anger was a question: Why would God give her sexual desires and not permit her to act on them? To not act on her desires caused her pain and anguish. Why would God wire her with sexual desires that she couldn't fulfill without sinning?

Being single and, thus, biblically restrained from acting out sexually does *not* mean you are less than as a human being. (I remind you that we serve a single, celibate Savior who definitely was *not* less than!) Also, we can live without sex as human beings, for it is not an essential appetite that must be satisfied like our appetite for food. If we think we have a right to fulfill ourselves sexually, we treat sexual fulfillment as an idol and a right.

According to Jesus, there is no marriage in heaven (Matt. 22:30), which means a single's struggle with unfulfilled sexual desires has an expiration date. Because there is no sin in heaven, we will think rightly, feel rightly, desire rightly, and act rightly when there, so even if we do have sexual desires in heaven, we will have them without sinning.

Desiring sexual consummation points us to the ultimate consummation when Christ returns for His bride. Our sexual desires are a form of body language, communicating spiritual truths about desire, fulfillment, and satisfaction. As Glynn Harrison puts it:

> Besides looking "into" our desires, we need to look "along" them—much as we would look "along" a signpost or the needle of a compass—to see where they point. . . . They are a divine homing instinct for the glorious union that lies ahead. And he [God] seeks from us the same faithful devotion, commitment, delight, and joy that he, through Christ, now finds in us.[7]

Being single and celibate as a Christian can make one feel out of place in churches full of married people and in a culture that mocks virginity. But if singleness is God's Plan A for you at this time, then celibacy is too. This does not make you less than, and it's not a waste of sexual desire because it points to the sufficiency of the One who created you and who alone can satisfy, fulfill, and complete you.

How Far Is Too Far?

In the Bible, we see three categories of how we relate to people: family, neighbors, and spouse. The only relational category in which sex is permitted is the marriage relationship. Since God declares incest to be a sin (Lev. 18:6–18), we are not to have sexual relations with our parents, siblings, children, grandparents, etc.

Anyone who does not fit the category of family or spouse falls under the category of neighbor. While we are to love our neighbor as ourselves (Matt. 22:39), we are *not* to have sex with our neighbor. The Bible calls this "fornication" or "adultery,"[8] and in Hosea, God even uses adultery as a metaphor for His people breaking faith with Him—that's how seriously He takes this sin.

These biblical categories of relationships have implications for dating and engagement, for people who are dating or engaged fall under the neighbor category. They're not yet husband and wife; therefore, sexual relations are not permissible. God's standard for purity in a dating relationship isn't any different from His standard for our neighbor relationships.

Consider the premise behind the "How far is too far?" question. Do we want to know the line, so we can do everything up to it? How does that perspective jive with 1 Corinthians 6:18's command to flee sexual sin? We make things worse for ourselves—not easier—when we inch closer to sin.

In 1 Corinthians 6:18–20 (ESV), Paul states:

> Flee from sexual immorality. Every other sin a person commits is outside the body, but the sexually immoral person sins against his own body. Or do you not know that your body is a temple of the Holy Spirit within you, whom you have from God? You are not your own, for you were bought with a price. So glorify God in your body.

What actions constitute sexual immorality? The Greek word for "sexual immorality" that's used here is *porneia*. It's an umbrella term for everything from adultery to prostitution to homosexuality and more. I find Kevin DeYoung's definition of the word to be helpful here:

> The simplest way to understand *porneia* is to think about the things that would make you furious and heartbroken if you found out someone was doing them with your husband or with your wife. If someone shook your wife's hand you would not be upset. If someone gave a casual side hug to your husband it probably wouldn't bother you. A kiss on the cheek or even a peck on the lips in some cultures might be appropriate. But if you found out another person had sex with your wife or saw her naked or touched certain parts of her body you would be furious. If you found another person made out with your husband or talked about sexual activities or made certain gestures you would be heartbroken. Why? Because these are all activities that are appropriate for a married couple but are inappropriate when

practiced outside of the lawful relationship of
a man and a woman in marriage.[9]

I've recently had two conversations with two separate
girls who went "too far" with their boyfriends, then attempted
to set boundaries only to totally disregard them. Knowing how
weak I am—how weak we all are—I appreciate the Bible's wisdom in urging us to treat "older women as mothers, younger
women as sisters, in all purity,"[10] and treat older men as fathers
and younger men as brothers.

Ephesians 5 considers the body of believers as Christ's
spouse. With this in mind, I should recognize that my boyfriend
or fiancé is already someone else's spouse—Christ's, and my
treatment of them should reflect this reality. How should I
treat someone else's spouse? How would I want someone else
to treat my husband? These questions help me remember
that any man I date isn't mine. He's not fair game because he
already belongs to someone else—Christ.

Commitment before intimacy—that's the biblical model
for relationships, and we see that with God's covenant with
Israel. The benefits of the relationship come after the commitment—the covenant—has been made. While there is a promise
to marry when two people get engaged, not all engagements
end in marriage. This is why it's helpful not to act like one
flesh when dating or engaged—because that's not your status
in God's eyes.

So if you're engaged, I urge you to hold on a little longer.
When you have his engagement ring on your finger, it's hard to
admit he's not officially yours, but honor your fiancé in light of
who he is today, not who you want him to be. Both of your bodies belong to Christ until *He* joins them, but as of today, you
are still two separate bodies. Trust Christ to join you together
in marriage when and if it's time. Again, *you can trust Him*. He
knows what is best for you and your body, and He cares for
you and your body.

What about Cohabitation?

"How can I know if my boyfriend and I are compatible unless we have sex and move in together?" If you've asked this, you're not alone. Or maybe your question is different. Maybe you're holding the line on sex but are wondering if it's okay to allow your boyfriend to sleep over. I especially see this with long-distance relationships where a boyfriend comes to visit, and he stays with his girlfriend since it's cheaper and more convenient. Or when dating or engaged couples stay in the same hotel room while on vacation.

At this point, I probably don't have to tell you that whatever the form cohabitation takes, if sexual activity is involved at all, it's outside God's design for sexuality (and therefore sin) since the two people are not married to each other. Let's say, though, that you're not having sex but are just sleeping over at your boyfriend's place. You're not technically breaking any biblical rules, right?

With what I'm about to say, I wish I could look you in the eyes, so you could hear my tone and see my expression to know I truly do desire what's best for you. There are plenty of things we're *permitted* to do—things that technically aren't sin, but consider the difference between what's permissible and beneficial.[11] How is sleeping over at your boyfriend's apartment *beneficial* to your walk with God? How is it spurring you on in your love for God? Would you rather scrape by in your relationships with your boyfriend and with God—or would you prefer to *flourish* in them? While doing what's beneficial is harder than merely doing what's permissible, the outcomes are *so much better*. Friend, I want to see you flourish, passionately pursuing the Lord and not hindering yourself in this by cohabitating with your boyfriend.

While we're on the subject of beneficial, we also need to consider our witness as believers. If our boyfriend or girlfriend spends the night, is this a *beneficial* witness to the world? Or does it look just like the world? Are we pointing people to Christ or away from Christ by our actions?

If God has a husband planned for you, I want that man to be someone who respects you, not tempts you. Someone who leads you to Christ, not sin. Someone who wants to partner with you in ministering to a lost world and who, therefore, cares what sleeping over looks like to your unbelieving friends and neighbors. If you're dating, does the guy merely check all the right boxes (Christian, member of a church, etc.) that make him permissible to date, or is he beneficial, leading you to flourish in your relationship with God?

Test-driving may work for determining what car to buy, but test-driving a potential spouse by living together does not work the same way. Why? Because going against God's design has consequences. If you want to act married, then get married! If you want the benefits of marriage, then commit and accept the responsibilities that come with it. But if you're not married, you're not within the bounds of God's design to enjoy one of the privileges of marriage—sex. And if you're the one who would commit but can't because the other party won't, let me say this friend to friend: don't waste your time playing house with someone who wants all the benefits without the commitment. Wait to build a home with someone who actually wants to make Christ the center of it!

What about Oral Sex?

While oral sex is another phrase you won't find in a Bible concordance, the fact that God designed sexual acts to be expressed within a covenant already implies that oral sex is off the table if you're not married.

One reason people engage in oral sex is because they consider it "safer," meaning women can't get pregnant from it. But both men and women *can* get STDs from oral sex. If a giver or receiver has an infection in any of the areas used, the infection can be transmitted.[12] Chlamydia, gonorrhea, syphilis, herpes, HPV, trichomoniasis, and even HIV are all common STDs a person can be infected with via oral sex. Therefore, while pregnancy might not be a consequence, given all the other consequences, oral sex isn't "safe sex."

Considering these STD risks, a natural question arises: is it biblically permissible for married couples to engage in oral sex if both spouses consider it a loving act that aids in intimacy and mutual pleasure?

Paul's words in Philippians 2:3–5 can help us here: "Do nothing out of selfish ambition or conceit, but in humility consider others as more important than yourselves. Everyone should look not to his own interests, but rather to the interests of others. Adopt the same attitude as that of Christ Jesus."

Husbands and wives should seek the good of the other; therefore, if one spouse feels uncomfortable with giving or receiving oral sex, the other spouse should value their feelings and, ultimately, do what is in the best interest of the other. As John Piper explains:

> . . . both the husband and the wife have the right to say to the other: I would like to [fill in the blank]. And both of them have the right to say: I would rather not [fill in the blank]. And in a good marriage, the biblically beautiful marriage, both of them seek to outdo the other in showing kindness.[13]

First Corinthians 7:3–4 describes how the body of a wife belongs to her husband and how the body of a husband belongs to his wife, but we should not weaponize this text, for example, to tell a wife that she must do whatever her husband wants sexually. That is a manipulation of God's Word. Coerced or manipulated sex is not selfless sex; it's abuse. With this, Dr.

Juli Slattery notes, "Some couples feel great freedom to include this [oral sex] in their lovemaking. For other couples, oral sex is a trigger of sexual abuse or pornographic images. The same act can be loving for one couple and harmful for another."[14]

God wants married couples to experience great plea-sure in sex, and the marriage covenant creates a safe place to experiment and to revel in each other. As married couples engage with each other sexually, communication is essential. How does giving or receiving certain sexual acts make them feel? Does oral sex make them feel safe, loved, and valued, or does it make them feel unsafe, gross, and devalued? Such con-versations can guide couples as they go deeper emotionally, sexually, and spiritually in their marriage.

What about Looking at Porn *with* My Spouse?

While sex being relational and covenantal already shows why pornography is a sin, a related question to porn has to do with the ethics of viewing porn *together* as a married couple. Can such a thing "count" as an expression of foreplay or even as an instruction manual if viewed together?

Just because you do something with your spouse does not mean that it honors the Lord. Whether separately or together, you dishonor your spouse and the Lord by viewing porn because pornography invites a third party into your mar-riage. Marriage is between one man and one woman. Even if the third party is digital, it is not your spouse. It is someone *in addition to* your spouse, and to look at people sexually who are not your spouse is lust. Viewing porn whether individually or together is a sin against God, your spouse, and the person/ people in the pornographic content. And have you considered that it also tells the wrong story about Christ and the church? As John Piper says, "this is a sin, a revolting sin. Revolting because it blasphemes Christ as if he needed sin to help him love his bride, because it celebrates the sickness and sin of the pornography industry, and because it insults the preciousness of a wife's heart and body by the one above all others who should cherish and nourish her soul."[15]

This doesn't just refer to porn that you find in a magazine or on a porn site. It also refers to the sex scenes in TV shows and movies. It is *not* God's design for you to watch someone else having sex.

Even when watched together, porn does not create intimacy in a marriage; it destroys it. It fuels fantasies that are out of bounds, fosters discontentment, adds a third party to the marriage bed, and creates an insatiable desire for more. No spouse can compete with the pornographic images on a screen; neither can porn compete with itself. This is why porn consumers escalate in what they view, constantly needing more provocative images or more novelty in order to get a fix.

Homosexuality, masturbation, BDSM, bestiality, sex toys, divorce, cohabitation, oral sex, pornography—we've covered quite a lot together! You're now *halfway* through our study of God's design for sex, so keep reading as we look next at the fourth characteristic of sex.

CHAPTER 8

Why Sexual Sin Is Sin: Sex Is Fruitful

WHEN GOD CREATED ADAM AND EVE, HE COULD HAVE DESIGNED sex to simply be an act of pleasure and bonding between a husband and wife, but He chose for sex to do more than that. He deemed it to be the method for human reproduction, so when He commanded Adam and Eve to, "Be fruitful and multiply and fill the earth" (Gen. 1:28 ESV), He was commanding them to have sex—and lots of it—in order to fill the earth with His image.

The ability to create life is one more way we reflect our Creator, the Giver of Life. Made in His likeness, we have the ability to make life. Human fruitfulness tells us about our God who is fruitful. It shows off what He's like—that He's a bountiful, creative, and powerful Designer. Isn't it mind-blowing that He made our bodies to tell this story?

Sex's Fruitfulness

In thinking about the fruitfulness of sex, I see it as being fruitful in two ways: (1) in strengthening the bond between husband and wife and (2) as a way to produce children. Knowing that God designed sex to be fruitful affects our understanding of sexual acts. For example, homosexuality lacks the ability to be fruitful, since both egg *and* sperm must be present for an embryo to form. Since masturbation is a personal, homosexual act, it too lacks the ability to be fruitful as does bestiality and the use of sexbots.

Sex isn't separated from procreation, but its fruitfulness involves more than just procreation. When Paul commands husbands and wives not to abstain from sex in 1 Corinthians 7:1–6, it's not necessarily because of the procreation element. Consider couples who have sex when the woman is post-menopause. Sex at that time no longer has the ability to be fruitful with regard to children, but it is still fruitful for the marriage. It deepens intimacy between a husband and wife, and it safeguards the marital union from sexual immorality. (It's not foolproof protection, but it is a safeguard.)

Should couples aim at procreation each time they have sex? I don't think so. However, knowing that intercourse can lead to children *should* affect how we view sex. It prevents sex from becoming an inward, selfish thing. Sex was not made for its own end. God designed it to be productive. It's productive in growing the relationship between the husband and wife. It's fruitful in that it can lead to the formation of human life. And it's profitable in that it tells the story of the fruitful, creative God of life.

Do you have pregnant friends who post pics of their baby bumps, updating everyone on when their little one is the size of a bell pepper, eggplant, or pineapple? They're literally bearing the proof of intimacy with their body. Our bodies demonstrate the truth that intimacy bears fruit, and our lives should do the same. In Galatians 5:22–23, Paul writes about the fruit of the Spirit in a Christian's life. The increasing presence of love, joy, peace, patience, kindness, goodness, faithfulness, gentleness, and self-control in our lives demonstrates a growing intimacy with God. Paul contrasts this with the fruit of the flesh: sexual immorality, idolatry, hatred, strife, jealousy, outbursts of anger, selfish ambition, envy, drunkenness, etc. (Gal. 5:19–21). With this in mind, what kind of fruit are you bearing in your life? Does it indicate intimacy with God?

Is It Wrong to Get Married but to Not Want or Have Children?

When I first started discipling college girls, the bulk of my conversations happened in a local Panera. I can still remember sitting in one of those multi-colored booths when I asked one particular girl—Bailey—what hindered her from trusting in Christ as her Lord and Savior.

Because of previous conversations, I expected her to mention evolution or the inerrancy of Scripture. Bailey's response? She was scared that if she became a Christian, God would call her to get married and have children!

Bailey did not want a family because she could accomplish more in her profession if she remained single and childless. To some degree, she's not wrong. Paul notes the benefits of singleness in 1 Corinthians 7, describing how the married person has divided interests. But Bailey preferred her plan to trusting God and His plan for her.

While infertility issues are out of our control, is it wrong for a Christian to get married, to not want children, and to take steps to not have children (via birth control pills, having your tubes tied, etc.)?

In the Old Testament, we see an emphasis on growing God's people via physical descendants. The creation commands to multiply and fill the earth with God's image are reiterated to Noah after the Flood (Gen. 9:1). God also emphasized the importance of physical descendants to Israel when teaching them that their obedience to His commands would lead to the experience of His blessings, including the multiplication of their people (Deut. 7:12–14).

With the first coming of Christ, humanity entered a new epoch. Instead of a focus on biological descendants, the New Testament introduces the concept of spiritual descendants. When Christ talks with the disciples about the kingdom of God, He tells how those who forsake their families for His sake would "receive a hundredfold now in this time, houses and brothers and sisters and mothers and children and lands."[1]

In Mark 10, Jesus teaches that those who forsake family for His sake will gain a family. I may not have biological children, but in obeying God's command to make disciples, I have spiritual children. Considering that the Great Commission is not optional, that all of us as Christians are commanded to make disciples (Matt. 28:19–20), the new covenant emphasizes the priority of growing God's kingdom via evangelism and discipleship. Sex remains the way in which humanity continues to procreate, but one does not become a Christian by being born into a Christian family. A person becomes a Christian by turning from their sin and trusting in Christ as Lord and Savior.

Currently, my lack of biological children means that I can disciple more girls than I could ever physically produce and parent. Spiritual babies and spiritual children need spiritual mothers, and many of the women I disciple have biological moms who are not spiritual moms. For this season, God has called me to be a spiritual mom to the young ladies He has placed in my life, and even if He later calls me to be a mom of physical children, the calling to be a disciple-maker—a spiritual mom—doesn't stop.

With this in mind, let's circle back to the question of whether it's wrong to be married and to *not* have biological children. Based on the New Testament's emphasis on discipleship, I don't believe it's a sin for married couples who are fully capable of having biological children to choose not to have them. There are those who would disagree with me here, and their arguments are valid. However, there's a place we both wholeheartedly agree: that it *is* a sin for believing couples—or for any Christian—to not make disciples.

With this, *how* such couples refrain from having biological children is important. For example, there's a difference between birth control that prevents sperm from fertilizing an egg and birth control that inhibits embryos from implanting in the womb (which is a form of abortion).[2] The Bible demonstrates that life begins at conception,[3] which is when sperm fertilizes an egg. Therefore, to interfere with an embryo's survival is to harm what the Bible *already constitutes as a human life*. This is why it's important to understand what type of birth control a doctor recommends and whether it's an abortifacient. The use of abortifacients essentially equates to having an abortion, but the use of condoms, diaphragms, natural family planning, or hormones that prevent ovulation (the production of eggs) or the egg and sperm from meeting are *not* abortifacients.

The topic of sterilization also comes into play here. Obviously, there are circumstances such as endometriosis or cancer where a woman needs a hysterectomy. But I urge caution for those who are considering a hysterectomy or vasectomy in order to simply avoid having children. To permanently incapacitate your capacity for procreation is an enormous act of presumption regarding God's will. What if you're married, get sterilized, your spouse dies, and you remarry and decide you *want* children? You would have made it impossible to change your mind if/when your circumstances change.

In contemplating birth control—both by avoiding conception and by voluntary sterilization—consider the motivation. Is your choice motivated by selfishness or pride? Do you view children as a burden? Do you want to avoid the challenges or pain associated with having and raising children? As John Piper urges, "If we decide to have children or not to have children, let it be worshipfully (because we have said yes to God's radical call on our lives), not selfishly (because it spares us some discomfort)."[4]

In an article on childlessness, Karen Swallow Prior shares about her infertility and how the contributions God has allowed her to make could not have been done if she'd been a mom. She states, "I can't help but wonder how the church and the world would look if infertility were viewed not as a problem to be solved, but a calling to serve God and meet the needs of the world in other ways."[5]

I have watched several of my friends struggle with infertility, and one such friend and I often discuss the correspondence between a single who desires marriage and a married woman who desires a child. Both have desires that rely—to varying degrees—on God's sovereignty. She can pursue various paths to help her grow a family, and I can pursue various ways of putting myself out there. But neither of us are promised by God to receive our desired results. Over and over, I have to examine whether or not I've made an idol of my desires. Today, where are my desires for a spouse or children in comparison to my desire to know, love, and follow God?

For those struggling with infertility, I pray you'll turn to God with your pain and be open-handed with God about your life. I pray that, through this, He will be your joy and that you will increasingly love and trust Him as you walk with Him. I don't know why you are in this situation, but I do know that God does not waste any of our experiences. You also have the promise of His presence (Ps. 139:7–12; Heb. 13:5), His love for you (Rom. 8:35–39; 1 John 4:9–19), and His sovereign, good plan for your life (1 Cor. 2:9; Phil. 1:6).

Some of you might have used birth control as an abortive agent. Whether you did this knowingly or unknowingly, we serve a God who forgives sin, so confess that sin to Him. Know that, if you are a Christian, He does not view you as sinner but as saint because of the blood of His Son Jesus Christ. You cannot change the past, but when you remember it, you can also remember what is true of you and your past because of your Savior. Do not wallow in the shame and guilt that Christ came to set you free from, but dwell on the One who is greater than our hearts, knows everything, and gave His life for the payment of our sins (1 John 2:1–2; 3:19–20).

What about Abortion?

A couple of years ago, God led me to serve with a pregnancy care center in Birmingham, and we recently hosted a live storytelling event where a selection of clients, volunteers, and staff told their story. Two moms courageously shared why they chose life, and the support they found that others lack, the help they were given that others do not receive, the options they were presented that others don't feel they have— it was a poignant reminder of why many women choose to end life rather than preserve it.

Some of you may currently be considering an abortion. While I do not know your circumstances, here's what the Bible teaches:

Life begins at conception. In Psalm 139:13–16, David notes how *God* is the One who knitted him together in his mother's womb. *God* knew before David's mother that life was growing in her womb. *God* saw David's unformed substance and knew how many days he would live. These truths demonstrate that an embryo and a fetus are more than just blobs of human tissue. Unborn human life is still human life; it just exists on one side of the birth canal as opposed to the other.

Human life has value. All human beings are made in the image of God (Gen. 1:26–28). This truth in and of itself gives inherent value to *all* human life, including the unborn.

Killing innocent human life is a sin. God is the Giver of Life,[6] and to kill a life is to assume God's role over life and death.

Therefore, abortion is an affront to God's authority as the Giver and Taker of life. Choosing to terminate life in the womb is equivalent to homicide, and the Bible calls murder a sin (Exod. 20:13; Matt. 5:21; James 2:11).

You have options. If you find yourself in an unplanned pregnancy, you have options other than abortion. If you're not currently able to raise a child, adoption is a viable alternative, enabling you to place your child in the care of a family that has the desire and means to care for him/her.

If you choose to parent, I encourage you to reach out to a pregnancy care center, if there is one in your community. Many have resources such as parenting classes, earn-while-you-learn programs, and support groups that can equip you and provide community as you parent. There also might be local churches in your community that have such programs, but even if there are none of these options where you live, at the very least, find a local church who will partner with you in discipling your child and where you can grow and find community as a Christ-follower.

To those of you reading this who have already had an abortion, know that there is grace and forgiveness in Christ. You have not done something outside of the realm of His forgiveness. We have examples of people in Scripture—Moses, David, and Paul—who were responsible for taking the lives of people, and God not only forgave them but greatly used them for His glory. He can do the same with you.

If you have sought God's forgiveness, you are forgiven. The question is whether or not you will *trust* in God's mercy and forgiveness. When our enemy, who is known as the Accuser (Rev. 12:10), reminds you of what you have done, will you allow him to blame and shame you, *or* will you acknowledge that, yes, you have sinned but that God has forgiven you and remembers your sin no more? Will you choose to believe that, as far as the east is from the west, so far has He removed your transgressions from you (Ps. 103:12)? Despite whatever you have done, you are dearly loved by God, and He has proved His love for you with His Son's death on the cross.

If you have had an abortion, have you taken the step to tell someone your secret? Have you talked about what has happened—to God and to other people (or at least one other person)? In *Suffering and the Heart of God*, counselor Diane Langberg describes three necessary responses involved in trauma recovery: talking, tears, and time.[7] It takes time and trust to verbalize what we have done and what has been done to us, but healing can occur.[8] However, healing won't happen if we're unwilling to bring to light what we've done. It won't occur if we're unwilling to feel our emotions related to the abortion. Grief, shame, guilt, despair, loss, anger—these feelings can be hard to bear. It takes time for wounds to heal, but verbalizing the reason for the wound and expressing emotions related to the wound contribute to the healing process. All of this takes time and must be done again and again, as long as the wound exists.

For believers in the local church, we can't leave all of the work to pregnancy care centers. We must *be the church*. We must be family to these women, receiving them, discipling them, and helping them raise their children in the faith. We shouldn't make things worse for them. They're already going to experience consequences for their choices, but our condemnation should not be among them. If God does not condemn His children (Rom. 8:1), neither should we as His people. If you are a Christian, you have experienced God's grace, and you are called to be an ambassador of His grace, a minister of reconciliation (2 Cor. 5:18–20). But we can't effectively promote that people can have a right relationship with God if we shun them for needing that right relationship in the first place.

>> CHAPTER 9 <<

Why Sexual Sin Is Sin: Sex Is Selfless

IMAGINE YOU'RE LIVING IN THE OLD TESTAMENT ERA. PICTURE yourself in a robe and sandals, living in a tent, cooking over a fire, and cleaning everything by hand. Visualize that you're in your mid-sixties and childless. Now, imagine that the Creator of the universe has appeared to your husband, promising that He would create a great nation from your husband and you—post-menopausal you.

However, a decade passes, and you're still childless. One day, you reach a point where you've had enough, so you approach your husband with a plan for how to have that promised son. Knowing the cultural custom of using a servant as a surrogate, you scheme to use your servant Hagar to provide an heir for your husband. While that means letting another woman into your husband's bed, it would only be until she was pregnant. Then your husband would finally have an heir. Problem solved, right?

Each time I read Genesis 16, I wonder if Abraham and Sarah even questioned what God thought about their culture's method of resolving infertility or if culture's norm had become their norm. Either way, Abraham and Sarah both demonstrate extreme selfishness in this text. They put their desire for a child above what was best for each other and their marriage. Blinded by their desires, Abraham and Sarah's plan also led to Hagar's violation. Simply because she was Sarah's maid, she was viewed as a means to an end, an object to be used rather than a person to be valued and respected.

In contrast to what we see in the Abraham-Sarah-Hagar debacle, God designed sex to be selfless, not selfish. Instead of pursuing what is best for me, I should pursue what is best for my spouse and for our marriage. Instead of seeking my own pleasure, I should seek my spouse's pleasure.

What about Conjugal Rights in Marriage?

In 1 Corinthians 7, Paul teaches about conjugal rights in marriage and notes: "A husband should fulfill his marital duty to his wife, and likewise a wife to her husband. A wife does not have the right over her own body, but her husband does. In the same way, a husband does not have the right over his own body, but his wife does."[1]

When Paul uses the phrase "marital duty" or "conjugal rights," some of you might feel like Paul is describing sex as a debt to be paid—like credit card debt or a mortgage. But that's not the connotation. Paul views sex as necessary to marriage, but it's viewed positively, as something you "pay" regularly but *want* to keep paying.

In this text, Paul clarifies that a spouse should not deny their partner's sexual desires, even on the basis of spiritual disciplines. If one spouse chooses celibacy, they resign their partner to celibacy, and according to Paul, this should not be. Such a fast must be mutual and only for an agreed amount of time for the purpose of prayer (v. 5). This command guards against selfishness dressed up in spirituality.

That Paul mentions nothing about children or procreation in this text is noteworthy and undergirds the importance of connection and pleasure experienced in sex by a married couple. The text also clearly communicates that abstinence should not be the norm in marriage. Other than the exclusion provided in 1 Corinthians 7:5, married couples should not deprive one another of sex. Does this mean, for example, that a wife can never say "no" to her husband but must give in to his desire for sex each and every time? Not necessarily. Mandated sex does *not* equal sex on demand. Living with your spouse in an understanding way means that you respect their no, but saying no should be the exception, not the rule. If you say no, consider why and plan for how you can say yes to your spouse soon.

Being selfless means not withholding sex if your husband doesn't do what you want, and it also means not faking how you feel. If you're pretending to like sex with your spouse, you're creating problems for yourself and your marriage. You might feel sexually incompatible with your husband, but you make yourself a sex object if you simply resign yourself to checking your husband's sex box instead of being honest with him about where you are. Being honest enables you to learn how to bring each other pleasure, but things will never improve without the two of you talking to each other about sex.

Being selfless requires sacrifice, and sacrifice costs. In Ephesians 5:28–30, Paul commands, "In the same way, husbands are to love their wives as their own bodies. He who loves his wife loves himself. For no one ever hates his own flesh but provides and cares for it, just as Christ does for the church, since we are members of his body."

A husband should love his spouse with *agape* (unconditional, sacrificial) love, and Paul compares a husband's love for his wife to two other types of love: a man's love for his own body and Christ's love for the church. By pointing the husband to care for his wife as Christ cares for the church, Paul reminds husbands that Christ gave His life for His bride in order for her to flourish. There's no greater cost than one's own life, and there's no greater demonstration of love than this (John 15:13).

As Mark 10:45 states, "the Son of Man did not come to be served, but to serve, and to give his life as a ransom for many." Serving requires selflessness. We must humble ourselves, thinking of ourselves less and our spouse more. Therefore, let the ethic of Philippians 2:3–4 direct our attitude toward sex in marriage: "Do nothing out of selfish ambition or conceit, but in humility consider others as more important than yourselves. Everyone should look not to his own interests, but rather to the interests of others."

Because of common grace, both unbelievers and believers can experience selfless sex, but when sex is used outside of God's design, it's automatically selfish. While selfless sex can seem like a contradiction, this is how God has designed sexual satisfaction to operate. As Daniel Heimbach observes:

> God has imbedded a paradox in how sexual pleasure works that helps restrain natural human selfishness. The more a couple focuses on pleasing each other, the more enjoyment each receives in return; and the more a person focuses on demanding his or her satisfaction, the less satisfaction is possible.[2]

Self-centeredness with sex can lead people to violate others for their own pleasure, even in marriage. Marital rape is a legit occurrence, but because the two people are married, forced sex has a cover under which it can hide. Whether or not you're married, coercive sex violates God's image-bearers. Being married does not entitle a person to sex on demand, for as counselor Darby Strickland observes, "Marriage does not equal consent."[3]

Such behavior goes against everything 1 Corinthians 13 teaches. Forced sex in marriage is not patient or kind. To demand, rant, lecture, or threaten until the other spouse gives in qualifies as abuse, not love. To disregard a wife's wishes about a particular sex act or the timing of sex demonstrates the husband's false belief that he has rights to his wife's body anytime he wants and in any way he wants.[4] Such a callous disdain distorts 1 Corinthians 7:3–4's teaching. To manipulate someone into sex with fear, guilt, or punishment flies in the face of a biblical definition of love, which "is not rude, is not self-seeking, is not irritable, and does not keep a record of wrongs."[5]

For couples where one spouse has a history of sexual violation, sex can be a hard or fearful thing. Sexual trauma as well as destructive choices made in the past can carry over into how you respond to sex. The whole idea of giving a spouse their conjugal rights can be joyful for some people but painful and truly a sacrifice for others. If these things describe you, seek help. Options can include sex therapy, trauma therapy, couples' therapy, a visit to your OBGYN, etc., but don't resign yourself to your current situation. Take a step to address it.

What about AR/VR Relationships and Pornography?

Although I grew up when Sega Genesis, Nintendo 64, and Game Boys were in their prime, I never was much of a gamer, and there's much of the gaming world I haven't explored. But after encountering several believers who have delved into sin via gaming and virtual reality products, the principles in this section will help in navigating the use of augmented reality and virtual reality products, even as technology shifts in coming years.

Virtual reality (VR) products simulate fictional environments, allowing us to interact with them in a physical way using particular electronic equipment. For example, we can play golf on a Wii, or a pilot can fly a plane in a simulation. Augmented reality (AR) refers to technology that allows us to interact and to experience the *real world* in augmented ways, creating a mirror world overlaying on top of the real world. For example, I've used AR technology when shopping by taking a picture of my living room, uploading it to the shopping site, and seeing what a rug looked like in the space.

While such technology can benefit humanity, it can also enable us to sin in new ways. Human nature doesn't change, even though technology will. We've used the printing press to print lewd descriptions, the camera to take pictures of naked people, the TV to watch other people have sex, the internet to view porn, and artificial intelligence to make sex robots. Now, VR and AR enable us to not just view porn but experience it.

While not everyone has VR or AR products, gaming allows people to meet other players from around the world. Our avatars interact with their avatars in a digital land. We can easily sin in our mismanagement of time using these products, but gaming, VR, AR, and any future platforms along these lines also provide opportunities for us to sin emotionally and sexually. Whether it's with the avatars created and operated by real people on the other side of a screen or whether it's with characters we've created within an online platform, we can act out our fantasies digitally, and VR and AR can take porn to a whole new level.

With VR, AR, and games, we can get lost in worlds (or versions of our worlds) instead of living life in the real world. As companies become adept at entertaining and hooking us into their products, we can become addicted to the experiences like how the near miss in a video game makes a player want to play again because they almost won. It also enables people to escape reality by entering a digital world where they can be drop-dead gorgeous and do what they want, unencumbered by the responsibilities and concerns of their present life. In the digital world of their own making, sickness is no more, financial problems are no more, and the effects of sin are no more. Who wouldn't want to spend time in a digital Eden like this?

While virtual relationships and digital sex do not have the same consequences as real-life relationships and sex, sex outside of marriage is a sin, and you create your own pornography when you use online platforms to create digital sexual experiences for yourself. Digital affairs are still affairs, and we shouldn't let technology supplant the one flesh union as God intended it to be experienced—in person with your spouse. God designed for sex to be relational, covenantal, heterosexual, fruitful, and selfless, and whether relationships are online or in person, we are to be holy as God is holy in how we engage in them.

As you evaluate your use of games or VR/AR technology, are you using them in a way that honors God?[6] Are you fighting the desires of your flesh, or are you using technology to indulge them? Are you cultivating contentment or discontentment in the way that you use these products? What does your use of tech convey about your beliefs about God and about yourself? Have you submitted your use of tech to Christ's authority? Does your use of these things reflect the way Jesus treats people?

If you struggle with this technology, effectively fighting sin in this area will likely entail getting rid of the technology itself. Don't underestimate your sin nature; instead, take your sin seriously by getting rid of the temptation. What's more important to you—your gaming device or your faithfulness to Jesus?

What about What We Wear?

Maybe you were fashionable as a teenager, but in the '90s, I wasn't. I couldn't pull off the tracksuits, MC Hammer pants, acid wash jeans, baby doll dresses, and grunge style like other middle schoolers. It probably didn't help that I incorporated Christian items in my outfits—you know, the WWJD bracelets and "Modest is Hottest" T-shirts.

Having grown up in church, my student ministry days involved True Love Waits, *I Kissed Dating Goodbye*, and many a talk on modesty. While being a Christian doesn't mean being frumpy instead of fashionable, being a Christian *should* affect what we wear and why we wear it. The Bible doesn't leave us without guidance in this area.[7]

Having charged Timothy with the task of pastoring the church in Ephesus, Paul wrote 1 Timothy so that this young pastor would "know how people ought to conduct themselves in God's household."[8] This purpose for the letter undergirds Paul's instructions regarding women's hairstyles and clothing in chapter two:

> likewise also that women should adorn them-
> selves in respectable apparel, with modesty
> and self-control, not with braided hair and
> gold or pearls or costly attire, but with what
> is proper for women who profess godliness—
> with good works.[9]

The context for this passage centers on how we're to conduct ourselves as Christians, and the passage has a missional emphasis because how we live affects what the unsaved think about God, the church, and the gospel. Paul begins by urging believers to pray for all people, particularly for government officials (vv. 1–7), for this exemplifies a peaceful, godly, and dignified life. Next, he urges men to pray without anger in their hearts or quarreling in their relationships (v. 8), and "like-wise," Paul urges women to exhibit restraint in verses 9–10. Although Paul does provide guidelines for women on how to dress, the text focuses more on the woman's character than her clothing because how we conduct ourselves affects our witness,[10] which is also why Paul exhorts women to do good works (v. 10).

Culturally, the elaborate hairstyles, gold, pearls, and expensive apparel that Paul instructed the women not to wear bespoke of promiscuity and even prostitution in the Roman culture. So for our culture, this doesn't mean we can't wear pearl earrings or braid our hair. Rather, we should avoid attire that communicates ostentation and promiscuity. Culture's standards of modesty and fashion will shift. But we don't dress for culture; we dress for Christ. Furthermore, we don't dress modestly for modesty's sake; we do so because we're patterning our lives after the modesty and humility of Christ, which includes far more than just our clothes (but does include them).

While Paul's instructions on what not to wear are culturally rooted, his guidelines for how to present ourselves are timeless. We should dress with propriety and self-control, and a lack of self-control in what we wear points to what we value. Ultimately, women who profess to worship God should dress themselves with good works (1 Tim. 2:10), investing more time in the development of character than in the curation of clothing.

We don't dress for ourselves. Everything we have—our bodies, our clothing, etc.—belongs to the Lord and is a gift from Him, and we must offer them back to the Giver and use them in ways that honor Him. In contrast, selfishness shows itself in using God's gifts for ourselves. We can be selfish in what we choose to do with our body, and we can be selfish in how we cover or don't cover our bodies. While fashionable outfits can be fun to put together, the real question is this: who is at the top of your mind when you dress? Yourself? A person whose attention you want? God? Do you ever think about how your attire represents Christ or what it might communicate to unbelievers?

As the biblical principle goes, the outside reflects the inside.[11] In other words, how you dress reflects what you treasure. Low-cut, tight, revealing clothing expresses more than your sense of fashion; it communicates what you value. Treasuring Christ should affect every area of your life, including your wardrobe. What does your wardrobe say about your worship? What does your clothing express about where you've placed your identity?

With all this talk about clothes, you might wonder if the Bible has anything to say about them on a grander level than just your outfit choices on a random Wednesday morning. And it does. After Adam and Eve sinned, God killed an animal and used its skins to make clothing for them. Their fig leaves— their attempts to cover themselves—were insufficient. The only sufficient covering for their guilt and shame was the covering God provided, which ultimately points to Christ's sufficiency in covering our sin. Adam and Eve sinned and needed to be clothed by the sacrifice, and Christ died naked on a tree in order to provide clothing for our guilt and shame.

Before sinning, Adam and Eve were naked and not ashamed (Gen. 2:25). But after sinning, they recognized their nakedness and felt the need to cover, even though they were married and the only two humans on the planet. God made them clothing, and in a sinful world, covering our bodies honors Him. We honor Him, and we honor His design for marriage by dressing modestly and not showing off our bodies to someone who is not our spouse. By giving clothing to both Eve *and Adam*, it demonstrates the importance of modesty and covering for *both* genders. Modesty isn't just an issue for women; it's important for men too.

This past year, my small group studied Galatians, and in this letter, Paul addresses two groups of people: the legalistic crowd who thought circumcision should be a requirement for Christ-followers, and the crowd who erred in the opposite direction, thinking the freedom they had in Christ gave them license to live how they wanted (Gal. 5:3–15). When discussing what we as Christians should and shouldn't wear, it's easy to swing one of these two directions. We can become legalistic about wearing shorts or skirts longer than our fingertips, not wearing spaghetti strap shirts, not wearing yoga pants, etc. Or we can think that freedom in Christ means we can each dress according to our convictions. ("You do you; just don't tell me how *I* should dress.")

With this, Galatians 5:13 states: "For you were called to be free, brothers and sisters; only don't use this freedom as an opportunity for the flesh, but serve one another through love." Just a couple of verses later, Paul urges the believers to "walk by the Spirit," for in doing so, they would not pursue their fleshly desires (v. 16), and he gives them examples of fleshly desires (sexual immorality, impurity, and sensuality or promiscuity), contrasting these desires with the fruit of the Spirit (vv. 19–23). What list better describes you—the works of the flesh list (vv. 19–21) or the works of the Spirit list (vv. 22–23)? Are the works of the Spirit—love, joy, peace, patience, kindness, goodness, faithfulness, gentleness, and self-control—evident in how you dress?

Ultimately, we as Christ-followers are to "put on" Christ (Rom. 13:14). We are to wear *Him*, and the fruit of the Spirit describes what that looks like. But we cannot look like Him or bear this fruit if we do not spend time with Him, which underscores the importance of growing our relationship with God.

God's Response to Our Selfishness

The stories we read in the Bible involve real people in history. Because so many of them seem like spiritual superheroes, it's easy to forget that. One man in the Old Testament who astounds me is Hosea, for I cannot imagine (A) being told to marry a prostitute, (B) experiencing the heartbreak of having your spouse repeatedly cheat on you, and (C) being asked by God to pursue, love, and care for the adulterous spouse.

It's one thing to read about this on the pages of our Bible; it was another for Hosea to live it. Can you imagine what he must have thought or felt as Gomer went away *again*, leaving him and the children in order to have sex with other men? How could he not have felt rejected, betrayed, unloved, hurt, angry, and grief-stricken? And can you imagine being told by the Lord to buy Gomer back from another man—*to pay* for her fidelity?

In all of this, the Lord tells Hosea up front that, in doing this with Gomer, he is presenting a picture of God's relationship with His covenant people (Hosea 1–3). Hosea, representing God, stands as a picture of selfless love, and Gomer, signifying Israel, represents the epitome of adultery—one who runs from that love in search of something better.

Yesterday, I had a conversation with a young lady about her sexual sin, and she admitted to not praying in an embarrassingly long time. When I asked why, she said it was because of shame and pride. Shame because of her sin and because it had been so long since she'd last prayed, and pride because she'd made it this far without Him (although we both acknowledged that the very fact she and I were having a conversation meant that she wasn't doing so well on her own).

With regard to her shame, she knew the Bible's truths that God wanted her to turn back to Him, but she didn't know *why* He would want her after knowing all she'd done. But that's the mystery and the beauty of the gospel. While we might have a hard time grasping how or why God would love Gomers like us, the Bible tells us that He does, and we can either choose to take Him at His word or not. Faith means trusting that God is merciful and gracious, even though we do not feel worthy of His forgiveness and love.

The Bible tells us that "We love because he first loved us" (1 John 4:19). In other words, God is the Hosea to our Gomer. An unwillingness to be selfless—being a Gomer—demonstrates a lack of understanding of God's love, for He is the God who—like Hosea—goes to His bride while she is in the midst of her sin. Rather than condemning or forsaking her, He saves her, loves her, restores her, and brings her home. God has shown us sacrificial, selfless, and unfailing love, and because of His love, He has provided both the example and the power for us to love others.

Did you know that this is how God pursues you, right there, wherever you are and whatever you've done? How can we receive such selfless love and not respond with gratitude and worship? Why wouldn't we take our cue from God and approach our relationships and sex lives with the same posture of selflessness? God sets the pattern of selflessness. Let's follow it.

>> CHAPTER 10 <<

Why Sexual Sin Is Sin: Sex Is Symbolic

THROUGHOUT SCRIPTURE, GOD INITIATES A RELATIONSHIP WITH people. God the Groom pursues His bride. The Old Testament covenants demonstrate this, and the story of Hosea and Gomer depicts this, as does the relationship between Solomon and his beloved. With Christ's death and resurrection, He's done what is necessary to win His bride, and He invites us into a never-ending relationship with Himself.

The one-flesh union of the husband and wife isn't an end in itself. According to the apostle Paul in Ephesians 5, it symbolizes something greater—the union of Christ and the church. Earthly marriage is the copy; the union of Christ and the church is the original. When God instituted marriage, He made it in the image of Christ the Bridegroom's eternal marriage with us, the church.

We've already discussed in chapter 5 how the roles of husbands and wives reflect the roles of Christ and the church, so as we consider what distinguishes a sexual act as sin, let's examine what the sexual act does to this picture of Christ and the church:

Premarital Sex, Extramarital Sex, Sexting, Crude Sexual Speech, Pornography, Prostitution, Oral Sex (outside of marriage), and Sexual Touching (outside of marriage): Christ does not have intimacy with someone He is not in a covenant relationship with. We do not experience the benefits of a relationship with Him without trusting in Him as our Lord and Savior. So, think about it: premarital sex and extramarital sex depict what? A situation where someone enjoys the benefits of covenant without actually having committed to that covenant in the first place. Said clearer: it pictures an unbeliever in an intimate relationship with God, having total access to the Lord they are still resisting. Sex outside of covenant pictures a non-Christian saying to God, "I want all the access and benefits that come along with You, but I don't want *You.*"

An intimate relationship with God is only possible for those who are in covenant with Him. Likewise, sexual intimacy with another person is only supposed to be available to those in a covenant relationship. All of the sexual acts listed in this section seek personal pleasure without marital commitment. With that, they exemplify lust, not love, and distort the picture of Christ's relationship with His church.

Fantasy and Erotica: A spouse does not think of another lover—real or fictional—for arousal, and this certainly is not how Christ relates to His bride. Reveling in such fictional storylines steers us away from our True Love and, if married, it contaminates our affections for our spouse. Instead of embracing one's current reality, fantasy imagines an alternate reality. Just as Christ does not want another bride, a husband should not fantasize about another partner. Just as the church does not need another Savior, a wife should likewise not fantasize about another husband.

Homosexuality and Masturbation: The relationship between Christ and the church depicts a relationship between two who are complementary but different. When it comes to the picture of Christ and the church, homosexuality depicts two of the same in the relationship, and as solo sex, masturbation leaves out one party all together.

Bestiality, Pornography, Sexual Fetishes, Sex Robots, and VR/AR Relationships and Sex: Instead of depicting the relationship between Christ and the church, these acts substitute other people, animals, or things as though Christ is replaceable or the church is replaceable.

BDSM and Sexual Violence/Abuse: With Christ and the church, there is a head and the body, servant leadership and glad submission. The "dominant" and "submissive" roles in BDSM pervert the biblical picture. Is Christ a sadist? Does He enjoy inflicting pain on His people? Is that how He shows His love for us? No! "But God proves his own love for us in that while we were still sinners, Christ died for us."[1] Christ demonstrated His love through self-sacrifice. In Ephesians 5:28, Paul commands husbands to "love their wives as their own bodies," which involves nourishing and cherishing them—not injuring them.

Transgenderism: Folks who seek to change their gender or to live according to a gender identity other than what God has given to them do experience genuine emotional distress (a.k.a. gender dysphoria), and while empathizing with the person's anguish, we also acknowledge that God did not engineer us with changeable chromosomes. Looking at the spiritual reality, the church cannot be Christ, and Christ cannot be the church.

Our sexual practices should accurately mirror the spiritual reality of Christ's union with the church. If you are considering a sexual act outside of marriage or even within marriage, ask yourself how that act depicts Christ's relationship with the church. Furthermore, is the act heterosexual? Relational? Covenantal? Fruitful? Selfless? A sexual act that aligns with *all six* of these characteristics of God's design honors the One who created sex.

To encapsulate all we've discussed about the six aspects of God's design for sex, examine the table in Appendix A at the end of the book. There, you see these six aspects of God's design listed side by side; and using these six characteristics, you can delineate whether or not a sexual act is aligned with God's design for sex.

What about Polyamorous Relationships and Swinging?

Although similar to polygamy, polyamory differs in that such relationships can occur outside of marriage. A poly group might consist of one married couple with other relationships—and even other married couples—as part of the triad, quadrad, etc. Such poly groups might look like one person dating two or three of the people in the group. With this option, think of a V with the primary person being the pivot and with the two other members of the triad being in relationship with the primary person but not with each other. For example, if Amber is the primary, she would be in a relationship with Tom and Sam, but Tom and Sam would not be in a relationship with each other.

However, a poly group might also consist of each person in the group being emotionally and sexually involved with the other members of the group. This would require at least some of the people to be bisexual; while the former option can be heterosexual or homosexual.

While polyamorous relationships involve two or more people who are okay with the relationship being open and involving other romantic partners, swinging is a subset of polyamory where spouses seek other couples for casual sex. Pushing for cultural acceptance of polyamory is a natural follow-up to the same-sex marriage movement, for if gender doesn't matter, why should the number of people in the relationship? Our culture has already redefined marriage according to emotional and sexual desire, so what's to stop it from expanding the definition to accommodate a desire for multiple partners, especially if "love makes a family"? To continue the argument, don't we have a right to be in a relationship that is satisfying to us, however we define that to be?

Polyamorists believe that one person alone cannot fulfill them. In a sense, they're not wrong. Another human being cannot fulfill us. Human marriage and relationships are not meant to fulfill you, so if someone is seeking satisfaction in a monogamous or polyamorous relationship, they're going to be disappointed.

Although partners in polyamorous relationships know and endorse each other's secondary relationships, it doesn't matter if your spouse is "fine" with it. Consensual, non-monogamous sex is still sex with people who aren't your spouse. Your spouse might give you consent, but God doesn't. He calls polyamorous relationships fornication, adultery, and sexually immoral.

With regard to how polygamy and polyamorous relationships reflect on the spiritual reality of Christ and the church, polygamy indicates that Christ could have many brides, more than just the church, or that the church could have many husbands, more than Christ. Polyamory doesn't require the marriage between Christ and the church and allows for Christ and the church to have additional relationships with others. None of these options represent gospel truth, which again demonstrates why we cannot rely on our feelings to guide our behavior.

The Story's End

The Bible begins with a marriage in Genesis 1–2 and ends with a marriage in Revelation 19. Upon engagement, the groom in ancient Jewish culture began preparing a home for his bride, and when all the arrangements were finalized, he would return for her and marry her, celebrating with a wedding banquet. We see this reality depicted in Jesus' parable of the ten virgins in Matthew 25, for the ten virgins (the bridesmaids of their era) were to watch and wait for the groom's return because that's when the wedding banquet would occur.

This is the picture Jesus presents at the Last Supper when He tells His disciples, "In my Father's house are many rooms. If it was not so, would have told you that I am going to prepare a place for you? If I go away and prepare a place for you, I will come again and take you to myself, so that where I am you may be also."[2] Jesus came to earth to pursue His bride, and His death and resurrection enable the relationship to occur. When Jesus ascended into heaven, He went away, but as He explained, He's coming back for His bride.

When giving thanks at the Last Supper, Jesus noted, "I will not drink of the fruit of the vine until the kingdom of God comes."[3] Four cups of wine were involved in a Passover meal: the cup of sanctification, the cup of interpretation, the cup of blessing, and the cup of consummation.[4] While Jesus drank the third cup (the cup of blessing), He committed to not drinking the fourth cup until the fulfillment—the consummation—of God's kingdom, which is a reference to the marriage supper of the Lamb.

At the Last Supper, Jesus inaugurated the new covenant with wine as a symbol for His blood that He was about to shed. With His blood, Jesus paid the dowry for His bride, purchasing His church at the cost of His own life.[5] With His blood, Jesus began a new covenant relationship, a marriage, and through His death, Christ made His bride holy, spotless, and blameless as Paul notes in Ephesians 5:25–27:

> Husbands, love your wives, just as Christ
> loved the church and gave himself for her to
> make her holy, cleansing her with the washing

of water by the word. He did this to present
the church to himself in splendor, without
spot or wrinkle or anything like that, but holy
and blameless.

Whenever we as believers partake in the Lord's Supper,
we "proclaim the Lord's death until he comes."[6] We affirm our
belief that Christ will return for His bride, and until then, we
remember and proclaim the gospel through the Lord's Supper.
When He returns, the Lord's Supper will be replaced with the
marriage supper of the Lamb. Currently, we come to the table
to remember Christ, but at the Messianic banquet, we will join
Christ at the table, celebrating a communion with Him that will
never end.

From the beginning, God knew the story He was telling.
In it, marriage exists for His glory, not ours. Through earthly
marriage, husbands and wives depict the truth that Christ
came to earth in pursuit of us to make us His bride, and we
as humans choose whether or not we'll enter into a relationship with Christ. When a man proposes to a woman, she can
either accept or refuse him. Similarly, Christ offers you the gift
of salvation (Rom. 6:23), and you choose whether to accept or
refuse Him. What is your response to Him?

>> CHAPTER II <<

How to Identify the Roots of Your Sexual Struggles

REMEMBER THAT TIME YOU GOT SHINGLES ON YOUR BIRTHDAY? No? Just me, then. See, at first I thought I had lice (especially since I had recently returned from a week of chaperoning at church camp and the itchiness and pain was primarily at the back of my scalp). A friend swore she saw no lice, but I did a RID treatment just in case. The symptoms remained, so I assumed I must have picked up bed bugs at the camp. I took antihistamines, applied hydrocortisone cream, and disinfected everything. But the symptoms persisted. Was it my hair products? Just in case, I bought different brands of shampoo and conditioner. But after all that, I only felt worse. Even Google and WebMD failed me! (Shocking, I know.)

Eventually, I shared my symptoms with a nurse, and her response was unexpected: "Ashley, do you think you might have shingles?" *No way. I'm too young!* But a visit to the doctor quickly confirmed she was right, and once I started taking the antiviral meds, my symptoms let up over time.

Why didn't any of my previous attempts to gain relief work? Because they didn't address the root cause of my symptoms.

As it turns out, we can make the same mistake when we attempt to alleviate our sexual struggles.

What's the Symptom? What's the Root?

Over the past decade of ministry, I've seen many young women address their sexual sin the way I tried to treat my shingles symptoms. Those with porn addictions get programs like Covenant Eyes, thinking that alone will stop their addiction. They might quit for a while, but sooner or later, they find other ways to view porn. Or a girl who masturbates will find a friend who agrees to be her accountability partner. She'll call the friend when she's struggling or confess to her after acting out, but her struggle with masturbation continues. The accountability partner helps some, but it hasn't stopped her from masturbating. Now don't get me wrong, Covenant Eyes and accountability partners are wonderful things, but they won't help you with your sexual sin unless you're *also* addressing the root of your sin.

Sexual sin is a symptom, not the root. Having sex with a guy, being in a homosexual relationship, fantasizing, reading erotica—these acts are sin, but they are also symptoms of sin. To effectively address the sexual sin, we must target the root.

What is the root? How do we identify it?

First, we need the Holy Spirit to give us discernment and strength. Identifying the beliefs and thoughts behind our actions requires self-examination, meaning we will see things about ourselves that are hard to face. We need reminders of God's forgiveness and of how He sees us as His beloved children, and while we may not feel like we can approach God because of what we've done or how we feel, we need His Word to speak truth to our feelings.

During the holidays, my mom and I gorge ourselves on Hallmark Christmas movies, and this year, I made a Hallmark Christmas Movie Bingo card where, as we watched a movie, we checked off boxes like "someone has a Christmas Eve deadline," "visits small town at Christmas," "main characters are rivals," or "has a classic misunderstanding in the last twenty minutes of the movie." But one such box on our bingo card is a classic Hallmark movie refrain that is *terrible* life advice: "follow your heart."

In contrast, Scripture tells us: "The heart is more deceitful than anything else,"[1] which is why we shouldn't necessarily believe what it says. While you shouldn't always follow your heart, you should analyze it. Emotions are helpful indicators of our internal world, so we should pay attention to how we feel and *why* we feel that way. When we give them this kind of attention, our emotions help us detect what we truly believe.

Consider a smoke detector. When it goes off, its incessant beeping warns you of a greater problem. Waving a fan in front of the smoke detector or taking out its batteries might stop the beeping, but you haven't identified or stopped the source of the smoke. Your emotions function like a smoke detector, and when you feel anxious, angry, lonely, etc., identify why and address what you find. While you shouldn't necessarily follow your heart and do whatever it desires, you should follow your heart in the sense of examining it and discovering its contents. Follow those feelings like they are smoke, and you'll eventually find the fire.

To help with this, let's walk together through the tool below to help uncover a root cause behind a certain emotion or sexual behavior.

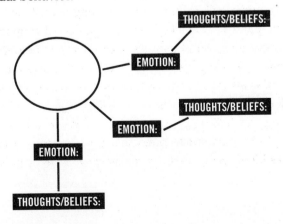

Step 1: The accompanying web contains a circle, which is where I start. If the issue is a sin struggle, I'll put the sin's name in the center of it. If I'm doing this simply because I feel a jumble of things, I'll label the circle with "today" since it's addressing where I am today. Or if I'm doing this with a girl and don't know exactly where she's going in the conversation, I'll put her name or initials. Essentially, the circle is my starting point.

Step 2: Next, I'll quickly identify all the things I feel, drawing a line from the center of the circle for each emotion I can identify. At this point, I simply record and label the emotions. When I'm doing this with a girl, I'll ask her to quickly identify each emotion with one or two words. If we're doing this because of a particular sin struggle such as porn or masturbation, I'll have her go back to the last time she was tempted, and we'll identify what she remembers feeling before acting out. The example web below contains an amalgamation of responses I've had from girls who struggle with porn and masturbation.

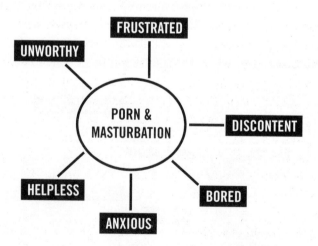

I often encounter girls who don't know what they are feeling. Perhaps they grew up in a dysfunctional family where they were not permitted to talk about their feelings or where they were not taught to be emotionally healthy. If you don't have the vocabulary to express how you feel, start with four primary emotions: anger, sadness, fear, and happiness. Look up synonyms of these primary emotions. For example, synonyms of anger include: annoyance, displeasure, exasperation, frustration, fury, hatred, impatience, indignation, irritation, rage, and resentment. If you know that you feel angry, do any of these synonyms better describe your anger?

Step 3: Once you have listed your emotions on the web, identify which you currently feel the most strongly. Use this emotion as your starting point for the next step.

Step 4: Starting with the strongest emotion, ask "why" and "what" questions to help you arrive at the thoughts and beliefs associated with that emotion. This is important because our feelings, thoughts, and beliefs affect each other.

Looking at the web, let's assume that discontentment is the strongest emotion, for it's often one that's listed when I ask young women what they were feeling before viewing porn or masturbating. At this point in the webbing process, I'll ask them what they feel discontent about. Maybe she mentions feeling discontent with singleness. She has desires to marry and have a family. Maybe there's a guy she likes, but nothing is happening on that front. Maybe there's no guy—even on dating sites—who's showing interest in her, or maybe the only guys interested in her are crazy. Furthermore, it's not unusual for evenings, especially the weekend, to be times when discontentment hits because that's prime date time that's being spent alone (or with your best friends Ben & Jerry).

When tracing the thoughts or beliefs behind an emotion, ask "what" and "why" questions until there's nothing left to say.

Consider yourself an investigator, exhausting every possible lead. With regard to the webbed example, press in on why the person wants to be married. Why does it bother her that no normal Christian guys seem to be interested in her? Why does it upset her to spend another Friday or Saturday night single?

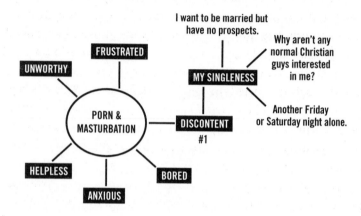

At this point, specifically attend to statements the person makes about what they think and believe about God, themselves, others, or how the world works.

Thoughts and Beliefs about God: If the girl desires to marry but currently has no prospects, what does she believe regarding God's plan for her or about singleness in general? Does she think that marriage is Plan A and singleness is Plan B and, thus, subpar to marriage? Does she claim Psalm 37:4, that God will give her the desire of her heart? What does she believe about God's love and care for her, specifically if He doesn't give her what she wants?

Thoughts and Beliefs about How the World Works: Maybe she thinks she'll remain unfulfilled, unhappy, incomplete, etc. until she's married. This already points to a potential idolatry of marriage, or at the very least, a lack of understanding about what the Bible teaches about singleness, marriage, happiness, and fulfillment.

Thoughts and Beliefs about Self: Looking at the sample web, questioning why normal Christian guys aren't interested in me might lead me to ask, "What's wrong with *me*?"

This week, a twenty-something girl called me to tell me about a recent blind date disaster. Her mom met a random woman while in the checkout line at Wal-Mart, and while talking, the moms discovered they both had single, adult children. (Are you cringing already?) Phone numbers were exchanged, and the guy actually texted the girl to ask her out on a date! While on the date, they ask typical get-to-know-you questions, and through this, she finds out he's done drugs. Many people have a past, but she wisely asks the follow-up question about recent drug use only to discover the dude uses LSD and wants to try ecstasy! (On the bright side, maybe her mom will stop giving out her number to random strangers?)

As she was relaying this to me (and I relay this with her permission), she mentioned spending the previous night crying to God, asking Him what's wrong with her that normal Christian guys aren't attracted to her. In fact, the only guys who seem to ask her out are ones who are addicts, have other issues, or just want to use her for sex. For this to be the case, she felt like something must be wrong with *her*.

At this point, it's easy to go down the rabbit hole of all the things that could be wrong with you. *I'm unlovable. I'm damaged goods because of my past. I'm unworthy of any good Christian guy's affection. I'm too much. I'm not pretty enough. I'm not smart enough. I'm too intimidating. I'm fat.* The list can go on. But what is it that you believe about yourself? How are your emotions speaking for you?

Thoughts and Beliefs about Others: When pressing in on the discontentment surrounding being single and spending another weekend dateless, comparison becomes easy. It seems like everyone around you is either dating, engaged, or married. Comparing myself to others and focusing on what they have versus what I don't have but want only serves to increase my discontentment.

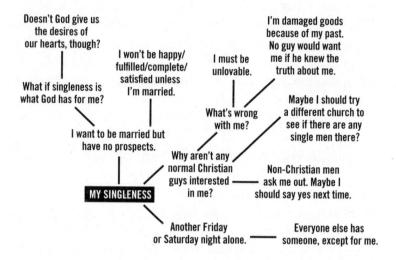

As the web shows, this is only what I've fleshed out regarding the *singleness* reason for discontentment. I haven't identified other possible reasons for feeling discontent, much less examined any of the other emotions originally listed!

If you haven't already picked up on this, webbing takes time, and it may not be something you complete in one sitting. That's okay! Begin by just listing the emotions, which you can quickly do in one sitting. That right there is a *win*. If you have the time, identify the strongest emotion and begin fleshing that one out. You might start on it, and come back to it a couple of hours or days later with more to add. Then, work on the next emotion, then the next. Or you might sit down and do the entire web all at once. Every person is different. But if this feels overwhelming to you, break it down into smaller, more manageable bits.

Block out time for this. Put it on your calendar or to-do list, so you can check it off. I've had some girls set timers for themselves, so they work on it until their timer goes off. Others who think the web is overwhelming will process these same things using bullet points, writing it all out paragraph style, or talking it through with a friend. Find a system that works for you. The point is to stop stuffing or avoiding your emotions and to identify what you feel and why. You cannot address sexual sin (the symptoms) without looking at the thoughts and beliefs behind the actions (the root).

Dispute False Beliefs with Biblical Truth

Our emotions and actions issue from what we love, which relates to our thoughts and beliefs. They function as consequences, so if I want to change how I feel and how I behave, I must address what I love and what I believe about what I love. If the loves and beliefs don't change, the emotions and behaviors won't change.

So, if we want to be transformed by God, we must examine the order of our loves and dislodge the false beliefs. I'm using "love" here as a shorthand for worship. Am I loving or worshiping another person more than God? My security more than God? Affirmation or affection more than God?

In our smoke detector analogy, our loves and beliefs are where the fire is. If we trace our emotions back to our loves and beliefs, we can do something about the fire that's burning down our house! Going back to the web on singleness, we see several examples of false beliefs, ignorance about God's truth, and a struggle with believing truth.

"I must be unlovable. I'm damaged goods because of my past." These statements express false beliefs about the self.

Are you familiar with *Jane Eyre*? Having been hired as the governess for Mr. Rochester's daughter, Jane initially thinks Mr. Rochester a widower, but she later discovers his wife to be alive yet insane. As Mr. Rochester confesses his love for Jane, she also acknowledges her love for him, but rather than give in to her feelings for him, she resolves to leave him. Mr. Rochester professes his desire to be with Jane, offering to make a home with her in France. While she did not doubt his passion for her and while she knew her own heart desired him, Jane could not avoid one simple truth: Mr. Rochester was a married man. In the book when she indicates her intent to leave, Mr. Rochester cries, "'What shall I do, Jane? Where turn for a companion, and for some hope?'"[2]

Jane's response? "Do as I do: trust in God and yourself. Believe in heaven. Hope to meet again there."[3] She resolved to "keep the law given by God"[4] rather than to follow her heart. What felt right to her, God deemed immoral. Her heart led her toward Rochester; God's truth led her away from him. So she fled Rochester's estate, leaving behind her job and the man she loved because she valued Someone more.

Like Jane, we must rely on God's truth rather than our feelings. With regard to our value and identity, what does the Bible say about us? We are image-bearers of God (Gen. 1:26–27); therefore, we have immense value and worth. While you have sinned and might have been sinned against, these things do not define you. God alone ascribes to you your value and worth, not the things you have done. Furthermore, if you are a Christian, you are a child of God (John 1:12)—that's your identity. You are loved by God (1 John 4:7–21), and He sees you as clean, righteous, and holy because Christ has paid the debt for your sin and has given you His righteousness.

Sister, you may *feel* unlovable. You may *feel* like damaged goods. But rather than trust your feelings, rehearse truth from God's Word about who you are. If this is an area in which you struggle, check out the accompanying sidebar on "What God Thinks about You," and let these verses be ones you study and commit to memory.

What God Thinks about You

- God made you in His image, and you reflect Him in a way that is utterly unique (Gen. 1:27).
- You are "fearfully and wonderfully made" by God (Ps. 139:14 ESV). You are how God designed you, and He does not make mistakes.
- Although you are a sinner, when God looks at you He sees the righteousness of Christ (2 Cor. 5:21).
- When you sin, you can confess your sin to God knowing that He will forgive you (1 John 1:9).
- God loves you (John 3:16; Eph. 2:4–9; 1 John 4:9–10, 19), and nothing—including your own sin—can separate you from His love (Rom. 8:31–39).
- You will fail, but Christ is sufficient (Rom. 7–8).
- God chose you to be His child (Eph. 1:4). You are wanted.
- God delights in you (Zeph. 3:17).
- God has saved you and given you a purpose (Eph. 1:4–10; 2:10).
- God has an inheritance for you—eternity with Him, and the Holy Spirit's presence in you serves as evidence of your salvation (Eph. 1:11–14).
- Christ sets sinners free (Gal. 5:1). Freedom from sin is possible because Christ's death conquered sin, Satan, and death (Eph. 1:19–23), and "we are more than conquerors through him who loved us" (Rom. 8:37). God calls you to live in light of this freedom (Gal. 5:13).

"What if singleness is what God has for me?" This question deals with what we believe about God, and as a singles minister, this question comes up a good bit in my line of work. For singles, it can be a struggle to trust God when He's not fulfilling the desire for marriage and family.

Maybe you're reading this wishing I had chosen a different example to flesh out because you're not single. If so, what's your faith question? Replace singleness in the following sentence: "What if _____ is what God allows to happen to me?" What did you put there? Infertility, chronic illness, the loss of a relationship, a prodigal child, etc.?

We don't know the future, but whatever happens, do you trust that God knows what is best for you? Do you trust that if singleness is His plan for you that He is worth it? That He will sustain you? That He is good? That His plan is best for you and the advancement of His kingdom? Being faced with singleness brings up these questions, and you must choose whether to trust God or to doubt Him and His plan.

What Does the Bible Say about God and His Plans?

"For I know the plans I have for you"—
this is the LORD's declaration—"plans
for your well-being, not for disaster,
to give you a future and a hope."
Jeremiah 29:11

But as it is written, "What no eye has
seen, no ear has heard, and no human
heart has conceived—God has prepared
these things for those who love him."
1 Corinthians 2:9

Oh, the depth of the riches and the wisdom and
of the knowledge of God! How unsearchable his
judgments and untraceable his ways! For who
has known the mind of the Lord? Or who has
been his counselor? And who has ever given to
God, that he should be repaid? For from him
and through him and to him are all things. To
him be the glory forever. Amen.
Romans 11:33–36

Going back to Genesis 3, the serpent initially questioned God's words, and from there, he attacked God's character, wanting the woman to think God was withholding good from her by not permitting her to eat the fruit. Does your estimation of good line up with God's? Do you trust Him when He says no to you? Do you trust the goodness, love, and care behind His no? Furthermore, do you trust God's goodness, love, and care for you when He permits hard things—even tragic things—to happen to you?

In times such as these, it can be hard to trust God because what we see, hear, and feel screams to us that God should not be trusted, but we must choose whether we will walk by faith or by sight. Will we behave according to how we feel or according to what God's Word says is true?

Conclusion

Situations happen in our lives, and we evaluate them, analyze them, and interpret them. Our beliefs about events can be true or false, rational or irrational. Either way, we think and believe something about what's happened, and we must identify what we're thinking and believing and assess it. When we act out in sin, we act the way we do because we believe the way we do and because we love the things we do. Our actions function as consequences of our thoughts, beliefs, and loves. While the web I've introduced in this chapter is not the end-all-be-all, it can assist you as a tool for processing what you're feeling and why.

If you're in the trenches right now in your fight against sexual sin, web when you're feeling tempted and examine what you're feeling and why. If you've acted out in sin, take time afterward to web, analyzing what happened, what you need to be aware of, and how you can respond differently next time. In seasons where you often feel "off" emotionally, you might web daily or several times a week because of the intensity of what you're facing, but in other seasons, you may not need to web as often. And remember, the point of all this—of identifying your false beliefs—is to throw those out and replace them with truth from Scripture. *You have a say in what you believe. When you evaluate what's going on internally and respond to your emotions, thoughts, and beliefs, you are choosing to let God's Word have the final say!*

Once you've identified your emotions and the thoughts, beliefs, and loves prompting your actions and emotions, what next? What do you do once you've identified the roots behind your behavior and replace them? How do you fight? That's where we're headed in the next chapter.

CHAPTER 12

Action Steps for Fighting Sin

THIS PAST YEAR, I DECIDED TO TRY MY HAND AT GARDENING; but before I could plant the flowers and shrubs in my yard, I had to uproot the weeds and stumps that were there. In the previous chapter, we learned how to identify and pull out our faulty beliefs—like weeds—and replace them with life-giving, true beliefs from God's Word. Now what?

Even new gardeners like me know that gardening requires effort to ensure the plants grow. I have to keep an eye out for pestilence, prune the plants, weed the flowerbeds, and fight against anything that would hinder the work I've done. Similarly, when you weed out false beliefs, replacing them with true ones, you want the true beliefs to take root and grow. So you need some follow-up steps—an action plan—to help you keep what's true "in there" and to fight off whatever might try to prevent it from taking root.

As we discuss practical ways to fight against sin, I have bad news and good news. Bad news first: what I'll relay in this chapter is *not* a magical formula. It's not a sure-fire cure. We will battle with sin to the day we die, but let me remind you of the good news: we fight against sin from a position of victory because of Christ.

How do I know this? Because passages like Ephesians 1:20–23 and Colossians 1:13–22 reveal God as all-powerful, raising Christ from the dead and setting Him above all powers and authorities. No one can defeat Him, and no one can undermine His work. What He wills to happen will, ultimately, happen. And if you are a Christian, you're on *His* team, the winning team. *You are on the team of the One who actually has the power to help you and who wants you to win!*

Romans 8 similarly shows us a God of victory. (You should go read it right now and underline the implications of God's victory for His people.) As a Christian, you have gone from being on the opposing team to being on God's team, part of His family. No one can succeed against God (v. 31). No one can accuse you because God justifies you (v. 33). No one can condemn you because Christ died, rose to life, and intercedes for you at God's right hand (v. 34). No one can separate you from God's love because "we are more than conquerors through him who loved us" (v. 37).

As we discuss biblical strategies for fighting sin, I pray you will keep these truths in mind. *Christ has defeated sin and can help you defeat it too. Lean into Him.*

What's Your Motivation for Fighting Sin?

I've made many mistakes along the way as I've discipled young women, and early on, God used my failure with one particular college student to teach me a valuable lesson about fighting sin. During that season, she and I met regularly, but I left each of our meetings feeling like she was worse off for it. While I would try to encourage her and speak truth to her, I felt like I was always giving her a list of things to do, which only served to increase her despair.

Recognizing my need for help as a disciple-maker, I met with a counselor, walked him through my last meeting with the girl, and asked him to identify what I was doing wrong and how I could help her instead of adding to her burden. He informed me that I was being a "gentle Pharisee" (my words, not his) in that I kept giving her Law when what she needed at the time was grace. While my words to her were prompted by love, they were misguided. While my counsel to her was not wrong because she should obey Scripture's commands, I erred in that I hadn't reminded her of the *whole* truth—of grace and love as well as obedience. I emphasized obedience to God when what she lacked was an awe and adoration of Him.

Striving for holiness didn't seem possible to her because of shame and guilt and also because she liked her sin. Instead of giving her a to-do list, I needed to cast vision for her, reminding her of God's worthiness, what it would be like to be free from sin's bondage, and why it's worth it to fight sin. Without such vision, she lacked the motivation to fight.

Love is a much better motivator than guilt. As I'm preparing for my small group's meeting this week, I know most of my girls struggle with consistency in studying Scripture, so it's something I'm about to address. Now, I could have a come-to-Jesus conversation with them where I berate them for choosing other things (like Netflix and sleep) over studying God's Word, *or* I could help them remember why God is worth choosing!

When you are tempted to sin, you can either focus on the sinful act that you want to do, letting thoughts of it consume your mind and increase your appetite for sin, or you can redirect your thoughts toward God's character, how He has worked in your life, and why it is worth it to resist temptation. In other words, you could look at your temptation. *Or* you could look at God. Cast vision for yourself. Pause right now and answer the following questions regarding your motivation for fighting sin:

- Why is God worthy of your resistance to temptation? What is His character?
- Why do you want to resist temptation? Why is it important to you?
- What result are you hoping for?
- What would life be like if you did not give into your sin struggle? How would your life be different than it is now?

Reflection on these things—*who* God is and *what* He has done—compels us to obey Him, for how can we refuse the One who loves us this much? Getting our eyes off our sin and onto Him is what ultimately motivates us to move out of sin and into obedience. So where are your eyes? Are you fighting your sin and obeying God out of duty or love?

Playing Offense and Defense

Although I wasn't that great, I played basketball for most of my grade school years, and in the sport, *offense* is when you attempt to score and *defense* is when you try to prevent the other team from scoring. For a basketball team to win, the players need to be skilled at both offense and defense.

When it comes to fighting sin, we need to play both offense and defense. Spiritually, what kinds of activities fall in the offense category and help us proactively fight against sin? At the moment of temptation, how can we practice good defense? While the list is not exhaustive, included below are a few suggestions for each area:

Offense	Defense
Studying Scripture	Casting vision to yourself
Memorizing Scripture	Rehearsing memorized Scripture
Prayer	Prayer

Being involved in biblical community	Reaching out to community for accountability
Being careful about your influences	Fleeing temptation rather than toeing the line
Identifying in advance how you can respond when tempted	Enacting your plan for how to respond when tempted

Our Playbook = Colossians 3

Colossians 3 has become my playbook for how to fight sin, for it addresses both offense and defense. As we examine this text, keep in mind that, as with basketball drills, the more you practice these skills the better you become at them.

1. Seek the things above.

So if you have been raised with Christ,
seek the things above, where Christ
is, seated at the right hand of God.
Colossians 3:1

What command does Paul give in Colossians 3:1? In your own life, what are you seeking? Is it Christ? What does it even look like to "seek the things above"?

In short, it encompasses all the things involved in growing your relationship with God: Bible study, prayer, memorizing Scripture, attending and serving in a local church, cultivating community with other Christians, sharing the gospel, discipling others, etc. Instead of seeking sin, we seek to follow and obey Christ.

Reflection Questions

- Based on what occupies your thoughts and time, what are you seeking in life?
- How can you take one step this week to grow your relationship with God?

2. Set your mind on things above.

Set your minds on things above,
not on earthly things. For you died,
and your life is hidden with Christ in God.
Colossians 3:2–3

In addition to seeking the things that are above, God directs us to *set our minds* on things above. Thinking back over today, what have you spent most of your time thinking about? What do you dream, daydream, or fantasize about?

If you're filling your mind with thoughts of bitterness, bitterness will ooze from you. If you spend your mental energy worrying, anxiety will consume you. If you constantly compare yourself to others, comparison and insecurity will dominate you. Can you see why Paul emphasizes taking "every thought captive to obey Christ" (2 Cor. 10:5)? But how do we do this?

If we're to set our minds on things above, we must identify the contents of our thoughts and filter them. Philippians 4:8 operates as our filter, guiding us in what should characterize our thought life: "Finally brothers and sisters, whatever is true, whatever is honorable, whatever is just, whatever is pure, whatever is lovely, whatever is commendable—if there is any moral excellence and if there is anything praiseworthy—dwell on these things." If a thought doesn't meet these requirements, then I shouldn't dwell on it.

Reflection Questions

- What has been the content of your thoughts today? How does it compare with Philippians 4:8?
- What mental pop-ups occur most frequently for you?
- If your mind wants to linger on a particular thought, particularly a sinful thought, examine why. What's the motivation? Why does your mind want to hover there?
- How can you respond when sinful pop-ups occur?

3. Put sin to death.

When Christ, who is your life,
appears, then you also will appear with
him in glory. Therefore, put to death what
belongs to your earthly nature: sexual
immorality, impurity, lust, evil desire, and
greed, which is idolatry. Because of these,
God's wrath is coming upon the disobedient,
and you once walked in these things when
you were living in them. But now, put away all
the following: anger, wrath, malice, slander,
and filthy language from your mouth. Do not
lie to one another, since you have put off the
old self with its practices.
Colossians 3:4–9

Obeying these commands is easier said than done, but Paul prefaces these commands with a motivating truth in verse four: "When Christ, who is your life, appears, then you also will appear with him in glory." Christ's second coming reminds me that putting sin away is something I will only have to do for a season. When Christ returns or when I die, I will no longer struggle with sin, for I will be sinless. At that time, we as Christians will share His glory. What hope!

While Paul gives a sample list of sins, what thoughts, attitudes, affections, or behaviors in your life need to be put to death? Putting sin to death might entail radical amputation in your life. Jesus gets at this in Matthew 5:29–30, "If your right eye causes you to sin, gouge it out and throw it away. For it is better that you lose one of the parts of your body than for your whole body to be thrown into hell. And if your right hand causes you to sin, cut it off and throw it away. For it is better that you lose one of the parts of your body than for your whole body to go into hell."

While I'm not suggesting you should literally gouge out your eye or cut off your hand, is there anything you need to eliminate from your life in order to put sin to death? For example, if your smartphone serves as your primary gateway to viewing porn, applying Matthew 5:29–30 to your situation might involve replacing the smartphone with a flip phone. That may sound radical to some of you, but what's more important—your soul or your smartphone?

How badly do you want to kill sin in your life? Do you hate your sin? Does it grieve you? If so, take the step to sever ties with whatever is enabling you.

Reflection Questions

- What in your life do you need to "put off"?
- Why should you "put off" that behavior?
- What people, places, and things trigger you to sin? How can you avoid such triggers?

- Do you need to apply radical amputation to a specific area of your life? If so, what?
- How can you go about doing that this week?

4. Put on the new self.

Do not lie to one another, since you have put off the old self with its practices and have put on the new self. You are being renewed in knowledge according to the image of your Creator. In Christ there is not Greek and Jew, circumcision and uncircumcision, barbarian, Scythian, slave and free; but Christ is all and in all. Therefore, as God's chosen ones, holy and dearly loved, put on compassion, kindness, humility, gentleness, and patience, bearing with one another and forgiving one another if anyone has a grievance against another. Just as the Lord has forgiven you, so you are also to forgive. Above all, put on love, which is the perfect bond of unity. And let the peace of Christ, to which you were also called in one body, rule your hearts. And be thankful. Let the word of Christ dwell richly among you, in all wisdom teaching and admonishing one another through psalms, hymns, and spiritual songs, singing to God with gratitude in your hearts. And whatever you do, in word or in deed, do everything in the name of the Lord Jesus, giving thanks to God the Father through him.
Colossians 3:9–17

What do laxatives have in common with putting off sin and putting on the new self? Taken to relieve constipation, a person ingests a laxative because they want their body to expel something. How do we fight—or expel—sin? By growing our love for God. With this "Spiritual Laxative Principle," we expel lesser loves (primarily our love for sin) by nurturing a greater love for God. This is how we avoid gratifying the desires of the flesh—by replacing old affections with a new, greater affection for God.[1]

Paul doesn't leave us wondering what the new self looks like, for in Colossians 3:9–17, he tells us what to put on: compassion, kindness, humility, gentleness, patience, forbearance, forgiveness, and love. None of these qualities happen accidentally. Sanctification takes time, and it doesn't always feel good. We seek the things above, set our minds on things above, put off sin, and put on Christ one day at a time. We might have days where we take two steps back, some days where we take a step forward, and other days where it's all we can do just to hold our ground. But overall, is the trajectory of your life one of obedience and growth? This trajectory depends on your daily choices—how you choose to think and act *today*. In light of this, "put on the Lord Jesus Christ, and make no provision for the flesh to gratify its desires.[2]

Reflection Questions

- Consider a temptation you commonly encounter. This week, how can you "put on the new self" in response to that temptation? What does it look like to replace that sinful behavior with a healthy, righteous one?
- Re-read the list of things Colossians 3:12–15 says we're to put on. Select one of these.

This week, how can you begin to grow in
this particular area?

A Practical Tool

As you take the principles from Colossians 3, use the following graphic organizer to assist you in applying these principles to your specific sin struggle.

1	2	3	4	5

On the scale, list your sin under the five. Since Colossians
3 talks about putting sin to death, write what needs to be to
put to death in your life. Under the three and four, list all of
the things that trigger you to sin. What's listed here may not
be sinful in and of itself, but if it leads you to sin, it's a problem
for *you*. For example, Netflix and Kindles are not sinful to have,
but if you cannot be on your Kindle without reading erotica,
then your Kindle falls in the three to four range and should be
something you "put off."

On the scale, one and two correlate with the "put on" commands as well as Colossians 3's commands to seek and set your
mind on things above. This might include spiritual activities as
well as practical ones such as "read or listen to the Bible each
day," "get seven to eight hours of sleep," or "exercise three to
four times a week."

As a check-in with girls, I'll often ask them to rate where
they are that day. Are they a four, which means they're triggered and on the road to giving into their sin? Are they a five
where they've acted out in the past twenty-four hours? Are
they a one or a two, heeding Colossians 3's commands and not

even thinking about their sin? With regard to accountability, I encourage young women to reach out to community for prayer and support if they're a three or a four. Don't wait until you're a five.

If you're an accountability partner, the 1–5 scale can help you with checking in and troubleshooting. Ask where they are on a scale of 1–5 and why they self-identify with that number. What things can they do right now to resist temptation? Many of the things they've listed as one or two behaviors can serve as replacement activities at this time. What do they need to resist temptation in this moment? Lastly, if they inform you that they've sinned, remind them of God's forgiveness and grace, and discuss what they can do differently next time they're tempted.

What Colossians 3 Says about You

Products usually come with warnings or disclaimers. For example, an iron might include the warning, "Do not iron with clothes on," and the manufacturer issues such warnings because some nitwit somewhere has tried to iron their clothes while wearing them and has burned themselves in the process.

Paul's instructions in Colossians give us an idea of what issues or sins were prevalent in the church at Colosse. When Paul tells them to "put to death what belongs to your earthly nature: sexual immorality, impurity, lust, evil desire, and greed, which is idolatry,"[3] it's likely that they were committing these particular sins, among others. But Paul also accompanies the commands in Colossians 3 with reminders about their identity and future:

- They have been raised with Christ (v. 1).
- They have died, and their life is hidden with Christ in God (v. 3).
- Christ is their life (v. 4).

- They will appear with Him in glory (v. 4).
- They have put off the old self and put on the new self (vv. 9–10).
- They are being renewed in knowledge according to the image of God (v. 10).
- In Christ, all people are equal in value and worth (v. 11).
- Christ is in all (v. 11). He's in them.
- They are chosen by God (v. 12).
- They are holy (v. 12).
- They are dearly loved by God (v. 12).
- They are forgiven by God (v. 13).
- They are called to one body with other believers (v. 15).

When we address our sin, we see the ugliness of our own hearts, which can be demoralizing. It's easy to read Scripture and to focus on our failure and insufficiency. Colossians 3's truths about our identity and future gird us up to combat against discouragement and shame. God wants us to remember these truths: that He chose us and wants us, even on our worst days (v. 12), that He sees us as holy (v. 12), that He loves us dearly (v. 12), that He forgives us (v. 13), and that He is in us (v. 11).

Sister, when you get discouraged in your fight against sin, reflect on how God has changed you. How has He grown you and worked in you? What does God think about you? What is true about your future because of Christ? Rather than gazing inward, look upward at the One who *will* complete the work He has begun in you (Phil. 1:6).

God may or may not take away your temptation, and when it comes to battling sin, the Navy Seals motto aptly applies: "The only easy day was yesterday." We will continue to face temptation as well as the consequences of our sin and the effects of other people's sin. But at the same time, God provides grace for us (James 4:6), and His mercies "are new every morning" (Lam. 3:23). God is making all things new, and He doesn't waste any of your experiences. Whatever your story is—and you may wish it were different—God can use everything in your life for your good and His glory. Your failures do not frustrate God's purposes, for nothing can hinder the fulfillment of His will.

CHAPTER 13

How to Go from Emotionally Unhealthy to Healthy

ALTHOUGH CASSIE SOUGHT ME OUT BECAUSE OF A HARDSHIP SHE was facing, I ended the conversation by praising God for how He'd worked in her during the three years I'd known her. When we first began meeting, God brought many things to light, and sexual sin with guys and an eating disorder topped the list. The more I listened, the more I discovered about Cassie's family, her past, and how she'd never learned how to deal with emotions. God exposed her sin struggles as coping mechanisms and began stripping them away, and things got worse before they got better.

As Cassie began to let herself feel emotions, a dam broke within her, and she could not control the ensuing flood of emotion. She went from stuffing her emotions to feeling and facing them, which was overwhelming, especially at the beginning. She also realized that she didn't know how to feel "negative" emotions without responding in a sinful way.

Spiritual growth entails emotional health, and Cassie could not effectively put her sin to death if she did not grow emotionally. Likewise, God wants you to grow emotionally. He wants you to accurately reflect His image, which means reflecting Him emotionally. Your spiritual growth will affect your emotional health, for you won't be able to grow spiritually without also growing emotionally.

Many factors contribute to a person's emotional stuntedness. For example, abuse, trauma, and dysfunctional upbringings can wreak all sorts of havoc on how a person forms emotionally over time. If this is your story, I'm so sorry. But there is good news: no matter what lies behind you, maturing both spiritually and emotionally really is possible. For all of us, there are things to unlearn as well as things to learn in order to become emotionally healthy.

God, Emotions, and You

Artist Andy Warhol often took a Polaroid of his subject to use as the starting point for a painted portrait. The famous people in Warhol's works—like Marilyn Monroe—are instantly identifiable, but his use of color either distorts them or accentuates their features.

With unhealthy emotions, we're like one of Warhol's works. We're recognizable as us, but the image doesn't match the real us as God designed us to be. Our unhealthy emotions and sin mar the image and distort it, but the more we grow in our relationship with God, the more we look like us as God intended.

He conforms us to the image of His Son, but this process isn't quick or easy. God doesn't want for your hurts to go unhealed or for you to hold onto sin. He knows your pain better than you do, for He's born witness to every hurt and every injustice you've experienced. He's not unaffected by your pain. He cares for you and is the One who "heals the brokenhearted."[1]

God could have made us without emotions, but our emotions are part of how we image Him. Because we have emotions, we can better understand Him and the gospel, for how could we understand God's delight and joy over us if we did not feel joy? How could we grasp God's wrath toward sin if we did not feel anger?

In giving us emotions, God also intends for us to glorify Him with how we express them. The Bible contains commands about what to feel and what not to feel, and glorifying Him with our emotions involves obeying these commands.[2] Thankfully God doesn't give us commands that He doesn't also equip us to obey.

Because of the Fall, sin disorders our emotions, but Christ's redemption extends to our emotions and helps reorder them once again. You might think, "I can't help the way I feel," but as a Christian, you *can* help how you feel. You're not at the mercy of your emotions. The very fact that He gives us commands about our emotions means that they can be regulated and submitted to His authority. As we "seek the things above" and "set your minds on things above,"[3] God sanctifies us, conforming us to the image of His Son,[4] for He wants us to accurately reflect Him with how we think, live, and *feel*.

In my first counseling class at seminary, my professor would often tell us, "Every emotion is a theological statement."[5] Every emotion reflects what we believe—about God, ourselves, others, how the world works, etc. We might *say* we believe one thing, but our emotions demonstrate what we *functionally* believe.

Our faith *should* affect how we feel. For example, when I sin, I should feel godly sorrow for having acted out against God. To clarify, none of this means that every day will be a spiritual high or that I will always feel close to God. As with any relationship, our feelings fluctuate, and we must remember the truth about the relationship and why we've chosen to be in it.

In *The Screwtape Letters*, C. S. Lewis writes about the "law of undulation,"[6] presenting life as a series of highs and lows. To think that Christians never experience depression, anxiety, or problematic emotions is to believe an emotional prosperity gospel. All of us will experience spiritually dry seasons for a number of different reasons, but will we continue to seek and obey Him, even when our emotions are lacking?

The Great Disconnect

As Christians, we read truth about God in the Bible, but growing our faith occurs as we apply biblical truth to daily life. In other words, we must leave the classroom and head to the lab (a.k.a. our lives). A couple of months before one of the hardest seasons of my life, God brought Hebrews 11:6 to my attention: "Now without faith it is impossible to please God." Although I studied that verse at the time, it wasn't until a couple of months down the road when I was nursing a broken heart that I began to understand what it means for my daily life.

If faith is required to please God, that means God will allow us to experience circumstances that grow our faith. Think of faith like a muscle. It either atrophies or grows, and growth occurs when the muscle is challenged to deal with higher levels of resistance or weight. Similarly, my faith can only grow so much in the classroom of reading the Bible. If all I do is gain knowledge about God, I become like the Christian version of a bobble-head doll where my head is disproportionately larger than the rest of my body. Life's circumstances serve as opportunities for our faith to grow, and application of biblical truth to daily life puts all that head knowledge to use.

The lesson I learned from Hebrews 11:6 was that I could choose to either walk by faith or by feeling. As a seminary student, I could explain Bible verses proclaiming God's love, His purpose in suffering, and His perfect plan for His children, but what I knew to be true did not *feel* true. I experienced a disconnect between what I knew and how I felt, and it was a season where God began connecting many biblical truths from my head to my heart.

Over the past decade of ministry, I repeatedly see young women who can talk about God's love, mercy, and grace all day, but believe He extends these things to everyone but them. I see women who try to control every area of life because of their own insecurities and fears, which drives friends, children, and significant others away because no one wants to be smothered and micromanaged in a relationship. In these situations, a gap exists between a person's beliefs and experiences. There's a disconnect between the head, heart, and hands—what we know the Bible says vs. what we feel and do. As Christians, how do we bridge this gap? How do we align what we know to be true with what we *feel*? To do this, we must first understand possible reasons for the disparity.

Not Dealing with Our Own Past and Woundedness

Because of the hurt Serena carried from her past, I often encouraged her to talk to a counselor, but she never would make the appointment because she didn't want to talk about her past. She likened it to scraping the scab off a wound, and to some degree, she was right. Talking about the past *will* bring things up. But if you want God to heal it, you must be willing to face it. If you don't deal with your past, you will experience a disconnect between what you know about God and how you live and feel, for you're continuing to hold on to your hurts instead of allowing Him to heal them.

Not Understanding the Gospel

As I disciple girls, I help them connect the dots between biblical truth and their daily lives. God doesn't intend for us to live compartmentalized lives where He has His box, and our work, sexuality, or money resides in other boxes, untouched by His influence. His authority extends to *every* area of our lives. Ignorance of biblical truth can sometimes be the culprit of our disconnect, but often, the issue can be application, not considering how the gospel applies to every area of our lives.

We don't just need the gospel for our salvation; we need it for our sanctification. As I've discipled young women, four aspects of the gospel tend to be common problem areas regarding the inordinacy between what we believe and how we live and feel: our sinfulness, the character of God, grace and forgiveness, and guilt and shame.

Our Sinfulness

First of all, if there's unconfessed or unrepentant sin in our lives, it hinders our relationship with God. While Christians can't lose their salvation, unrepentant sin does disrupt our fellowship with the Father because we're rebelling against Him. Our disobedience to God prevents us from getting what we know about Christ from our head to our hearts.

Rather than claiming responsibility for our sin, we often prefer to shift the responsibility to other people or to our circumstances. Two common receptacles for our blame include our genetics (nature) and our environment (nurture), but while our biology and our environment do influence us, they do not determine our behavior. As long as we try to shift the blame for our sin rather than taking responsibility, we will experience a disconnect between what we say we believe about the gospel and how we live and feel.

The Character of God

What images or words come to mind when you think about God?

Do you view God as loving and caring? Do you perceive Him to be judgmental, harsh, unpredictable, or strict? As A. W. Tozer so famously said, "What comes into our minds when we think about God is the most important thing about us."[7] Relatedly, when I'm listening to girls share their story, I'll commonly ask them about their view of God, and the most surprising but enlightening answers I've heard are that God is oppressive and wrathful.

Oppressive: Because God didn't approve of something she felt pleasure in (namely, her sexual sin), one young woman considered Him oppressive. Furthermore, if He didn't want her to engage in that sin, He would remove the desire. If He loved her, He wouldn't want her to suffer, and He would take away her struggle and her suffering. This view places on God the demand for freedom—either freedom from a sin struggle or the freedom to live how she wants without feeling guilt for it.

Wrathful: For one college student, if God wasn't taking away her suffering and sin struggle, she questioned His care for her as well as her own salvation. Was He turning His back on her? Would she come to the end of her life only to find she'd been deceived about her salvation? Instead of being chosen and wanted by God, would she be judged by Him, a recipient of His wrath instead of His mercy?

Can you see how such views of God would affect someone's emotions? Does a discrepancy exist between what the Bible says about God's character and how you live and feel? Do you allow your circumstances to interpret God, or do you use Scripture's teaching to interpret your circumstances?

Grace and Forgiveness

(*Star Wars* spoiler alert!) In *The Force Awakens*, Kylo Ren kills his father Han Solo. Han tries to convince Kylo Ren to leave the dark side, but rather than believe he can be free of his pain and return home, Kylo Ren thrusts a lightsaber into Han, killing him.

Later in *The Rise of Skywalker*, Kylo Ren faces another opportunity to choose light over darkness, and as he agonizes over this decision, he has a vision of his father. Kylo Ren feels guilty for all of the evil he's done in his past, but haunting him the most is the murder of his father. In the vision, Han urges his son to come home, but Kylo Ren remarks that it's too late for him. But in a Han Solo-esque way, the father assures his son of his love, leaving the prodigal son with a choice: will he believe his father's love and forgiveness or will he allow the burden of his sins to drive him further into darkness?

Like Kylo Ren, we face a decision. Our heavenly Father offers us love, forgiveness, grace, and mercy. The sacrifice of His Son stands as proof of this. Will you accept what He offers, applying this grace to yourself? If you don't, you will drive yourself into despair because you can never be good enough, and all of your attempts to be good will only frustrate you as you increasingly realize your own sinfulness.

A discrepancy between what we say we believe and how we live and feel will exist as long as we try to earn God's forgiveness rather than trusting the grace He offers. He intends for His grace to be received, not achieved. Earned grace is not grace at all, for grace is when you're given something you don't deserve.

Colossians 1:22 teaches: "But now he [Christ] has reconciled you by his physical body through his death, to present you holy, faultless, and blameless before him." *Christ* does this work. *Christ* makes you holy, faultless, and blameless. *Christ* does for you what you cannot do for yourself. If you are a

Christian, do you try to prove your worthiness to God instead of enjoying the fact that He has made you worthy through Christ? You might know in your head that you're saved by grace through faith in Christ, but are you living like it?

So many women I meet feel like they're not enough and question whether they can ever be enough. Sister, God doesn't have some standard for "enough-ness" He's requiring you to meet because He's already met that standard in Christ. He just calls you to believe it.

But This Guilt Won't Let Up!

In addition to asking girls what comes to mind when they think about God, I'll also invite them to give me adjectives that describe how they see themselves. In one such conversation, the young woman offered the following descriptions: whore, cutter, [expletive]ed up, manipulative, and piece of [expletive].

Some of these labels stemmed from her involvement in sin. She saw herself as guilty of sin, which is true. She is guilty of these sins as well as others, and we must recognize our sin and confess it. But she also saw the wrongs she'd done and had defined herself in light of them.

Next, I asked her to identify what the Bible says regarding how *God* sees her, and she promptly recited: redeemed, forgiven, adopted, and child of God. This sister knew what the Bible says about her identity. But how she felt about herself didn't line up with Scripture, and behaviorally, she lived out the labels she felt rather than what the Word says. If we do not understand what the Bible teaches about guilt and shame and apply those truths to ourselves, we will experience a disconnect between what we say we believe and how we live and feel.

What is true about our guilt and shame? In the Old Testament era, the Israelites worshiped God at the temple, and a room called the Holy of Holies existed in the innermost part of the temple. This room contained the ark of the covenant, and among other items, the ark contained the stone tablets bearing the Ten Commandments. Because it was the place of God's presence, the high priest could only enter this room one day a year—the Day of Atonement. The purpose of this annual visit was to sprinkle the blood of the sacrifice onto the mercy seat, which was the golden lid on the ark of the covenant.

In light of this, the Holy of Holies never received a spring-cleaning. If sprinkling blood on the mercy seat was the only thing the priest could do in the Holy of Holies, then the room and the ark never got cleaned, which means years of dried blood accumulated on and around the ark.

How does all of this relate to your guilt and shame? When God looked down on the ark of the covenant, He saw the stone tablets inside bearing the Law, and He remembered all of the ways His people had broken His laws. But because of the blood sprinkled on the mercy seat, when God looked down at the ark, He not only saw the Law and how His people had broken it—He saw it through the blood of the sacrifice. As a result, the people experienced atonement, their debt of sin being satisfied by the blood of the sacrifice.

With the Day of Atonement, God provides an object lesson for us of what is ultimately true in Christ. When God looks at you, He knows your sins better than you do. He knows all of the ways you have broken His laws and all the ways you will break His laws in the future. But if you are a Christian, when He looks at you, He sees you through the blood of the sacrifice of His Son.

Christ not only paid your sin debt; He credited *His* righteousness to your account. You are no longer guilty; you are pardoned because Someone paid your debt for you. As Colossians 2:13–14 states: "And when you were dead in trespasses and in the uncircumcision of your flesh, he made you alive with him and forgave us all our trespasses. He erased the certificate of debt, with its obligations, that was against us and opposed to us, and has taken it away by nailing it to the cross."

In light of this glorious truth, when we feel condemned by our sins, let us remind ourselves:

> "When Satan tempts me to despair
> And tells me of the guilt within
> Upward I look and see Him there,
> Who made an end of all my sin.
> Because the sinless Savior died,
> My sinful soul is counted free;
> For God the Just is satisfied
> To look on Him and pardon me."[8]

But What about the Shame I Feel?

This addresses our guilt, but what about our shame? While guilt acknowledges that we've done wrong, shame has to do with how we view ourselves because of what we've done or because of what's been done to us. Reinforcing our sense of shame is our Enemy, the "accuser of our brothers and sisters" (Rev. 12:10). While God calls us by our name, Satan calls us by our sin. While we may have done the things he accuses us of, he does not recount the *whole* story. He fails to mention what is true because of Christ.

All non-Christians are enemies of God, but Jesus died for His enemies (Rom. 5:10). Not only that, He died so we could go from being His enemies to being part of His family. For those who trust in Christ for salvation, our identity is no longer as God's enemies but God's *children* (Rom. 8:16–17). On the cross, Jesus took our shame, and He shares His glory with God's children. He gives you honor to replace your shame.

Shame makes us feel unclean, untouchable, and disgusting. It leads us to feel undeserving of hope and causes us to think we're unusable in ministry. But God doesn't call us to look inward for our value or identity. He calls us to look to *Him*. Our relationship with God makes us clean and acceptable, not because of what we've done but because of what *He's* done!

God knew what He was getting when He invited you into His family. Nothing about you is unknown to Him. However unworthy you feel, God the Father offers to cover your shame. Similar to Luke 15's story of the prodigal son, you did not earn your heavenly Father's compassionate response or generous gifts. You do not deserve to be treated as a child of God. None of us do because we are all sinners. That's why the gospel is such good news!

Sister, if you trust in Christ for salvation, He replaces your shame with honor. You can come before Him fully known and fully loved. You do not have to fear Him, for He does not condemn His children. He does not accuse us because He's already forgiven us. He does not reject us because He's already accepted us. He does not despise us because His Son was despised for us. He does not reject us because His Son was rejected for us. We are unworthy, but His Son is worthy. *He* has made us clean in Christ. *He* has made us acceptable in His sight by giving us *His* honor and glory. *He* has given us a new name and a new identity. *He* has made us new.

When it comes to how you view yourself, who will you believe—yourself or God?

> But you are a chosen race, a royal priesthood, a holy nation, a people for his own possession, so that you may proclaim the praises of the one who called you out of darkness into his marvelous light. Once you were not a people, but now you are God's people; you had not received mercy, but now you have received mercy.
> 1 Peter 2:9–10

How Do We Grow Emotionally?

If we recognize that a disconnect exists between what the Bible says about God and how we live and feel, how can we change and grow emotionally?

First, **go to God with your emotions**. Be honest with Him about your questions and feelings. He already knows, and He's big enough to handle all that you think and feel.

Psalm 22 provides a helpful guide for us in what it looks like to go to God with our emotions. King David felt abandoned by God, and throughout the first half of the song, he waxes and wanes. He begins with a lament about his circumstances (vv. 1–2); then, he reminds himself of God's character and His faithfulness to His people in history (vv. 3–5). David bemoans his situation, describing how others ridicule him (vv. 6–8); then, he rehearses God's care for him in his past (vv. 9–10). Following this, David petitions the Lord for deliverance (vv. 11–21).

David doesn't have it all together in Psalm 22. In fact, he's a hot mess. But he goes to God with the mess, not waiting until it's all sorted before approaching Him. Like David, we can be honest with God about how we feel, and as he models for us in this psalm, we should also remind ourselves of what is true about God's character, God's faithfulness to His people in the past, and how He has worked in our own lives.

In addition to going to God with how we feel, we should **understand our emotions and what's behind them**. Use the webbing tool we've discussed to better understand why you feel the way you do. Examine how your emotions are speaking *for* you as the shorthand of your beliefs, and question how your emotions are speaking *to* you, deluding you. Don't be ruled by your emotions. As Edward Welch notes, "The stronger the emotion, the harder it is to hear the truth. . . . Strong emotions have much in common with delusions. Delusions insist on their interpretations despite clear reason, all contrary evidence or consensus among friends for a different interpretation."[9]

If we refuse to deal with our emotions, we miss out on His ability to transform them.

God wants to restore you. To do this requires acknowledging the damage that's been done and the emotions associated with the pain. While we want to either ignore our emotions or wallow in them like a pig in a pigpen, God wants to make us whole.

As we understand what's behind our emotions, we should **mortify ungodly emotions and beliefs**. This underscores Colossians 3:5's command to "put to death what belongs to your earthly nature." As you identify what thoughts and beliefs lie behind your emotions, if there is any sin, confess it to God and put it to death.

While mortifying ungodly emotions and beliefs is one side of the coin, the flip side of it involves **cultivating godly emotions**. We don't just get rid of ungodly emotions; we replace them.

Emotional health requires knowing and growing with the One who made your emotions. He is our example of what emotional health looks like, for He expresses His emotions without sin. Sin does not taint His thoughts and emotions the way it does ours. While we will not feel perfectly in this life, His Spirit resides in us, and His sanctifying work extends to our emotions.

God desires our obedience in our thoughts, actions, *and* emotions. As we **listen to truth and renew our minds**, it affects our emotions, for as we base our lives on truth, we will begin to choose faith over feelings and understand our feelings in light of Scripture. As Paul David Tripp states, "My self-perception is as accurate as a carnival mirror. If I am going to see myself clearly, I need you to hold the mirror of God's Word in front of me."[10]

Lastly, we grow emotionally by **taking care of our bodies**. You are a human being, not a machine. What you eat, how much or little you exercise, and how much you sleep affects you. Your physical health affects your emotional health. How are you stewarding the body God has given to you? Are there any changes you need to make regarding exercise, sleep, diet, or stress management that would better position you to mortify ungodly emotions and cultivate godly ones?

Take heart, Christian. Our emotions *can* be trained, educated, overcome, and improved. They are not runaway horses operating outside of God's sovereignty. *God is able.* His Spirit in us enables our obedience in *all* areas of life, and one day when we stand in God's presence, all will be made right. We will think and feel perfectly, for nothing about us will be disordered by sin or its effects.

CHAPTER 14

How to Walk Alongside Others in the Battle

GOD CHOOSES UNLIKELY PEOPLE TO DO HIS WORK. HE PLUCKED Abraham out of obscurity to make him the father of many nations and the patriarch of Israel. From a burning bush, God called Moses—a murderer—to confront Pharaoh and lead God's people out of slavery. He appointed Jael, a nomadic housewife, to use a hammer and tent peg to kill the captain of a mighty Canaanite army. He selected fearful, fleece-laying Gideon to deliver Israel from their Midianite oppressors. He incorporated not just one—but three—*Gentile* women of faith into the Messianic line (Tamar, Rahab, and Ruth). He chose David, a shepherd boy, to defeat a Philistine giant and be king over Israel. He sovereignly enabled Esther, a normal Jewish woman, to be selected as the bride of King Ahasuerus and to, thus, be in a position to save the Israelites from genocide. He chose Mary, a young Jewish woman of no consequence, to be the mom of the Messiah. He handpicked a motley crew of men, including a tax collector, a zealot, and fishermen, to be His disciples, and He intercepted Paul, a persecutor of Christians, calling him to write a huge chunk of the New Testament.

Most—if not all—of these people were ill-equipped to do what they did. But what they accomplished did not rest on their abilities or accomplishments but on the strength of the One who selected them for service. For His glory, God uses the weak to shame the wise and to demonstrate His power.

I say this to encourage you. When the girls I discipled first started telling me about their sexual sin, addictions, and trauma, I felt in over my head. In leading me to walk alongside these young women, God called me to step out of my comfort zone and into unfamiliar territory. What did I know about discipling people as they pursue sobriety, identify roots of sin, and allow God to heal their trauma wounds? But God provided through His Spirit, His church, and His Word. I wasn't prepared on the front end, but He equipped me along the way, leading me to depend on Him because I sure couldn't depend on myself. I *knew* He had me operating out of my depth. Through it all, He kept me on my knees, begging Him for wisdom, discernment, patience, and strength.

I did not do things perfectly, though. Remember my experience with shingles? Well, from August to April of that school year, I had shingles, lice (which I got from a movie theater seat), the flu, *and* cracked ribs! Over the years, God has used my physical health and how my body responds to stress as a self-check for when I'm unhealthy and on the road to burnout. During that Job-like year of one health challenge after another, God led me to read and reflect on work, rest, recreation, and emotional health, and I emerged from that season, making several changes to how I approach ministry and structure my time.

The Health of the Alongsider

Your spiritual health matters.

According to Jesus, loving God is the greatest command-ment (Matt. 22:37–39), but do you prioritize this in your daily life? Do you delight in Him, or is everything you do out of a sense of duty or obligation to Him? I'm *not* saying you'll always feel a spiritual high or excitement, but cultivating a greater love for God means putting your worship of Him ahead of your service to Him. It means soaking in Scripture *for yourself*, applying it to *your* life, and not just studying it to prepare for the next thing you're teaching. It means wanting Him for Him and not for what He can do for you. It means talking to Him and not just about Him.

If you knew you were about to die, what would you want to express to your closest friends? Called the "Farewell Discourse," John 13–16 records Jesus' final conversation with His disciples on the night before His death. At this last sup-per, Jesus emphasized the importance of staying connected to the True Vine: "Remain in me, and I in you. Just as a branch is unable to produce fruit by itself unless it remains on the vine, neither can you unless you remain in me. I am the vine; you are the branches. The one who remains in me and I in him pro-duces much fruit, because you can do nothing without me."[1]

Later in this conversation, Jesus describes how His follow-ers are to "go and bear fruit and that your fruit should abide."[2] What is this fruit that "abides"? The context suggests that the fruit is converts. Your union with Christ should lead others to unite with Christ; but in order to love people rightly, I must love God more. My loves and priorities must be in the right order, for disorder in my worship inevitably leads to disordered rela-tionships. My relationship with God affects my relationships with others. As Puritan pastor John Flavel notes, "The believer is in spiritual danger if he allows himself to go for any length of time without tasting the love of Christ and savoring the felt comforts of a Savior's presence. When Christ ceases to fill the heart with satisfaction, our souls will go in silent search of other lovers."[3]

As you consider the reflection questions below, evaluate where you currently are in your love for God and why you are there. Next, identify one step you can take to grow your relationship with Him *this week*. Let that take precedent over reading this book, for your relationship with God is the most important relationship of your life.

Reflection Questions

- What does studying the Bible currently look like in your life?
- What does prayer currently look like in your life?
- Spiritually, who teaches and leads you? Who are you learning from?
- Who prays with you, and who prays for you?
- Are you keeping short accounts with the Lord, confessing sin to Him and repenting of it?
- What does thanksgiving look like in your life?
- What next steps do you need to take to grow your relationship with the Lord?
- What is currently motivating your ministry efforts?

Your physical health matters.

During my year of shingles and sequential health issues, I realized I had little to no margin in my life. I operated at a pace that was unsustainable, but it wasn't until sickness slowed me down that I even had the time to recognize the unsustainability of my life. I felt guilty for resting when I could be doing, feeling the pressure to maximize every spare bit of time. I identified in myself a lack of trust in God, which was evidenced by how I didn't trust Him to work when I wasn't. I also acknowledged using busyness as a filler to avoid feeling empty and alone.

With setting aside a day of rest, God gave humanity a boundary, indicating our need to recover energy after six days of expending it. On the seventh day of creation, God also looked back at what He'd made, evaluating it and enjoying it (Gen. 2:1–3), and we miss opportunities for reflection if we constantly press forward without taking time to look back. In addition to a day of rest, God commanded Israel to give the *land* a Sabbath every seventh year (Lev. 25:1–7), and taking that year off from farming and pruning reminded Israel that just because something could be maximized doesn't mean it should be.

In this journey, God has showed me that much of what I thought was "resting" was actually escaping. The two are *not* synonymous. Rest leaves me refreshed and ready to return to work, but when I escape, I'm increasingly disinclined to reengage, mostly because I spent the time numbing out or putting my felt needs first. Escapism means I've misused energy rather than recovered it,[4] but God designed the Sabbath for our *rest* from work, not our escape from it.

After my shingles season, I became more diligent about exercise and the types of food I consume. I established blocks of time in the week when I'm "off," which means not meeting with girls or doing work, and during these times, I give myself permission to put my phone on "do not disturb." I use up all my vacation days every year, and I began incorporating retreat days into each semester where I take time to evaluate and pray about all areas of my life. I identified the things that are my "yes" in life, so I know what to say "no" to (and I'm getting more comfortable with saying "no"). Instead of filling up every day of my week, I created margin, which leaves room for the unexpected things that come up as well as space to hear from God.

Like me, you're a human *being*, not a human doing. God has given you margins to live within, and you're on the road to burnout if you live as though you don't have limits. We must steward our availability and resources as we minister to others. Doing so is loving ourselves as well as the people we're ministering to, for we are better ministers, friends, and mentors when we rest, have off time, and do not allow the needs and pain of others to be the driving force of our schedule. Living under the tyranny of the urgent easily leads us to forget why we're living in the first place. The second greatest commandment should never surpass the first in our lives.

Reflection Questions

- Are there any changes (diet, exercise, sleep, etc.) you need to make in order to be a better steward of your body and health? If so, how can you begin making those changes this week?
- What activities refresh you? How can you incorporate these with some regularity in your schedule?
- What does rest look like in your life? When are you "off"?

Your emotional health matters.

If you've ever spent two seconds around a campfire, you know that the "campfire smell" tends to linger in your hair and clothes. Bearing people's stories can be that way too. It's a privilege to listen to people, of course, but that doesn't mean it's easy to be a human receptacle for stories of rape, abuse, neglect, addiction, and sexual sin. These stories—like the campfire scent—often stay with me long after the conversation ends. I've experienced nightmares, intrusions, insomnia, concentration issues, and other symptoms of compassion fatigue that are unavoidable if you do this work long enough.

Walking alongside others puts you in the blast radius of their lives, and being a steward of their stories comes at a price. It exacts an emotional toil, for one doesn't bear burdens with people without being affected by them. To not feel or be affected is *not* the goal. I hope I never get to a point of being undisturbed by the ravaging effects of sin in people's lives. Stories of suffering and sin *should* affect me. It reminds me that this is not the way things should be, and it points to how things *will* one day be made right because of Christ.

But how do we take care of ourselves emotionally as we walk alongside others, especially when their stories affect us emotionally? Prioritizing my relationship with Christ and my physical health cannot be understated here. Additionally, taking notes on my conversations with girls enables me to record the salient details on paper, letting go of them as I jot them down. I can off-load the details rather than carry them, and note-taking also enables me to review pertinent information before meeting with the person again.

For deep dives, scuba divers shouldn't *quickly* swim to the surface. Because breathing out of a pressurized tank affects nitrogen levels in the body, divers must incorporate decompression stops into their ascension in order to avoid decompression sickness. During heavy conversations with girls, I try to incorporate decompression time into the last couple of minutes of conversation to help them transition from talking about weighty things to going about the rest of their day. Usually, I'll ask them what they have planned for the rest of the day or week to transition the conversation to a lighter topic. I've done everything from go on a walk around the block with a girl to playing a quick game of Bananagrams to help someone shift from our conversation to what's next in their day. I also make sure they have a plan of what to do or who to call, if that's needed.

But they're not the only ones who need decompression time. I need it too after they leave. Webbing my emotions, note-taking, reading a book, going on a walk, cleaning, watching a light-hearted movie or TV show (even for just 10–15 minutes) helps me to decompress. Sometimes, I can do it right after the conversation, but that's not always possible. Usually, my decompression time is during my commute or at night, and sometimes, I'll even visualize the conversations as books that I'm closing and putting on the bookshelf or that I'm putting a bookmark in and stacking on my desk to come back to at a later date. I'll talk to God about these "books," telling Him my thoughts and feelings and lifting up various requests.

As we strive to be emotionally healthy alongsiders, Philippians 4:4 commands us to "rejoice in the Lord always," and verse 5 reminds us that "the Lord is near." The next verse tells us not to worry but, instead, to take our requests to God, pairing them with thanksgiving. Rejoicing, giving thanks, speaking my requests to God, and remembering His nearness—in doing these things, I'm not ignoring the suffering I hear but am choosing to dwell on God and what is good. I'm remembering the bigger story of God's work in redemption history. Instead of zooming in on the suffering I encounter, I'm zooming out to remember how God has been at work in the past and how He is working toward the recreation of all things. The work is hard, but it is *possible* when I remind myself of the cross and the future Christ bought for me on that tree. The same goes for you. As you help others, you're in the blast radius, yes, but you know the One who took the blast in full form and paid for all of it already. *He absorbed far more than you ever have to. He can see you through this.*

Reflection Questions

- How do you lead when you're going through a hard season? When should you persevere in leadership, and when should you take a step back?
- How do you process what you feel?
- Are there any unhealthy coping mechanisms that you need to address? If so, how can you begin to replace unhealthy habits with healthy ones?

Your relational health matters.

As en vogue as being "independent" is in our culture, the truth is, none of us truly are. We depend on our cars to turn on every morning, so we can get to wherever we need to go. We rely on farmers to grow food for us to eat, and we need air in order to breathe.

While you may not like the idea of being dependent, you need a support system as you walk alongside others, and the people you're helping need a support system that involves more than just you. Support systems can include family members, friends, mentors, counselors, and coworkers, and they take time and initiative to develop. You need this if you're single as well as married because, as wonderful as your spouse is, he cannot be your everything. Keep in mind that you can be social and around a lot of people, but that doesn't necessarily mean you have a group of people who support you.

Are you known? You may not be equally known by everyone in your support system, but you should have people who know your story, your secrets, and your struggles. While some may not know the gritty details, you should be able to authentically admit your needs and ask for prayer or help. We lose out when we pretend to be fine, and we hinder our brothers and sisters from obeying the "one another" commands in Scripture when we refuse to let them bear burdens with us.

It's also dangerous to cling too much to our support system. When we overly depend on ourselves or others, we're not depending on the only One who is self-sufficient, all-powerful, and who can bear the full weight of our brokenness. People do not sufficiently substitute for God; instead, they should point us to Him. Balance is key here.

If you're walking with someone while they're suffering, the relationship will likely be one-sided. You may also find that, while you're life-giving to the person you're walking alongside, they're not life-giving to you. God uses you in each other's lives, but not in the same way. They may not mean to you what you mean to them, and that's okay. God calls me to minister to many different girls, but that doesn't mean they all have to be my buddies. We should adjust our expectations of relationships, for they won't all be reciprocal.

With all the outpouring I do, especially with a ministry job, I need "exhale people"[5] in my life. These are people I can kick back with and exhale when around because they're not peppering me with church questions or asking me to wear my counseling hat in my off hours. With these friends, I can speak candidly because I know they love me, warts and all. We all need these people in our lives. Sometimes these people are mentors; while other times, a mentor is harder to find. Such is the ebb and flow of life. In either case, spending time with "exhale" people is valuable.

But even with "exhale people" in your life, you're going to feel lonely at times, for even your deepest relationships cannot fully satisfy you. But when we are with God in heaven, we will no longer experience loneliness, for all of our relationships will be as God originally intended. Whether loneliness is your constant companion or an emotion that pops up in various seasons, loneliness is not eternal, and ultimately, it helps us remember that Christ is our constant Companion (Heb. 13:5), opening the door to knowing God more deeply than we did before.

In *The Preacher's Wife*, Reverend Henry Biggs character demonstrates a dangerous tendency we can easily have when doing "the Lord's work"—putting it before our family and our own health. Be on guard against crucifying your family for the sake of ministry. You may not have a ministry job, but it can be easy to put serving opportunities and discipling relationships ahead of your spouse or children. While there will be occasions where family time may be sacrificed because of ministry, this should not be the norm. Investing in others should not come before investing in your spouse and children.

As you walk alongside others, your relational health matters. You need a support system and relationships that are life-giving, especially as you minister to people who drain you. If all of your relationships have some sort of power deferential where you're the one in authority, that's a problem. You need people who know the real you and who live out the one another commands with you. Use the reflection questions below as you evaluate your relational health and the current relationships in your life.

Reflection Questions

- Who refreshes you? Who can you be transparent with?
- How do you deal with conflict in your life?
- Who are you specifically investing in? What does that currently look like, and what does it need to look like?
- In what ways do you need to be equipped?
- What dreams and prayers do you have for the people you're walking alongside?
- When seasons of loneliness occur, how can you cope in God-honoring ways?

CHAPTER 15

How God Heals Our Brokenness

WHO KNOWS THE REAL YOU?

Who knows how you're actually doing? The struggles you're facing? The sin you're battling? The suffering you've endured? Does anyone know?

On more than one occasion, I've heard young women voice a fear of church people knowing their sin struggles. These women eagerly seek assistance from therapists and recovery groups, finding no judgment there for their past and present, but they lack the same assurance about the church and question whether the local church is a safe place to air their dirty laundry.

These women don't have it all together, and they feel like that's visible to everyone. They feel shame being around people who are consistent in Bible study when spiritual disciplines are hard for them. They're still grappling with guilt and shame for what they've done or are questioning if God can be trusted after what He's allowed them to suffer. They fear the looks of revulsion that might occur if they tell their struggles to other Christians. They wonder if the church will cast proverbial stones at them the way the Jewish religious leaders did at the adulteress in John 8. If they tell of their sin, is *that* how they will thereafter be known and thought of—by their scarlet letter? For a sinner, God's people can often be scarier to face than God Himself.

The concerns of these young women are valid. How many Christians have shamed a struggler instead of helped them? *The Scarlet Letter* is a classic for a reason. Hester Prynn isn't the only one who's been shunned by a church or community for her sin. How quickly God's saints often forget that they too are sinners in need of God's grace!

I get the wariness some of you might have about the local church. You've got battle scars from having grown up in legalistic churches and from encountering people who do not act like the Christ they claim to follow. But please do not project your experience with one church onto all churches or your encounters with a few Christians onto all Christians. Don't give up on the body of Christ.

Why? Because God has designed the local church to be a people who help each other increasingly love God, reflect His character, and participate in His mission. While God certainly does use therapists, recovery groups, books, etc. in our healing journey, these do not substitute for His Word, His Spirit, and His church. They can be used in conjunction with them but not in replacement of them. If you want to be all-in on God's healing, you need to go all-in with His people. To better understand this, let's see what 1 John has to say.

Fellowship and the Family of God

There's a therapist in my community with an office pillow that has the following quote cross-stitched on it: "Everyone needs someone to bear witness to their story."

True, isn't it? We all want to be known. We want people to hear our story. We want people to know and accept us. And there's a reason for that—God built us that way. He fashioned us to flourish in community. Our healing cannot occur without this.

In the midst of false teaching and confusion over what's true about Jesus and salvation, John wrote the letter we know as 1 John in order to give believers assurance of the truth and confidence about their salvation. If you are someone who struggles with doubt about your salvation, God included an entire book in the Bible to address this. He wants His people to have assurance of where they stand with Him, for He doesn't want His children to grapple with doubt about His affections and His salvation.

In his opening remarks of the letter, John invites his readers to experience fellowship with the apostles and with God (v. 3), but this fellowship is only achieved by believing the truth about Christ, the "word of life" (vv. 1–3). The One who is Life stands as the final authority on how to achieve eternal life, and throughout Scripture, God reminds us that our salvation rests not on our perfection but on Christ's.

In verse 3, John introduces the word *fellowship* into the discussion, which occurs four times in chapter 1. Since I'm someone who grew up in a church with a "fellowship hall" that hosted everything from Wednesday night suppers to bridal showers, let me clarify what this particular Greek word for fellowship (*koinonia*) actually means: a "close association involving mutual interests and sharing."[1]

Before Christ, we're born into a literal family, but we lack a spiritual one. Spiritually, unbelievers are slaves to sin and children of wrath (Eph. 2:1–3). But upon our salvation, God "undoes our unbelonging"[2] by bringing us into His family as His sons and daughters. Jesus states this Himself in Mark's Gospel:

> He replied to them, "Who are my mother and
> my brothers?" Looking at those sitting in a
> circle around him, he said,

> "Here are my mother and my brothers!
> Whoever does the will of God is my
> brother and sister and mother."
> Mark 3:33–35

> "Truly I tell you," Jesus said, "there is no one
> who has left house or brothers or sisters or
> mother or father or children or fields for my
> sake and for the sake of the gospel, who will
> not receive a hundred times more, now at this
> time—houses, brothers and sisters, mothers
> and children, and fields, with persecutions—
> and eternal life in the age to come."
> Mark 10:29–30

Jesus redefines family. Maybe you've had a wonderful family of origin, or maybe you lack a sense of belonging because you were abandoned, mistreated, neglected, abused, or orphaned by those closest to you. But Jesus promises family to those who follow Him, and Ephesians 2 clarifies who constitutes that family—those who turn from their sin and trust in Him. When we come to God, He connects us to an entirely new community—one that walks with us through the highs and lows of life, including our struggles with sin. As Sam Allberry states: "Following him means an abundance of spiritual family. Nature may have given us only one mother and one father; the gospel gives us far more."[3]

In all of this, bear in mind that community or fellowship with one another is a massive benefit for the Christian, but it's not the only reason God brought us into His family. To make community the point of Christianity would neglect the centrality of Christ and the urgency of His mission. Fellowship is one of the wonderful *by-products* of believing biblical truth about Jesus and living out that truth together.

The New Testament does not teach Lone Ranger Christianity. In fact, the New Testament contains over fifty descriptions of how we're to interact with "one another":

- "Love one another deeply as brothers and sisters" (Rom. 12:10)
- "Live in harmony with one another" (Rom. 12:16)
- "Serve one another through love" (Gal. 5:13)
- "Carry one another's burdens" (Gal. 6:2)
- "Bearing with one another in love" (Eph. 4:2)
- "Be kind and compassionate to one another" (Eph. 4:32)
- "Forgiving one another, just as God also forgave you in Christ" (Eph. 4:32)
- "In humility consider others as more important than yourselves" (Phil. 2:3)
- "Do not lie to one another" (Col. 3:9)
- "Do not complain about one another" (James 5:9)
- "Confess your sins to one another" (James 5:16)
- "Pray for one another" (James 5:16)
- "Be hospitable to one another without complaining" (1 Pet. 4:9)

While I've provided only a small sampling of the one another passages, you get the idea. These "one another" commands depict what it looks like to live as members of God's family, and by obeying them, you help undo the unbelonging that fellow brothers and sisters may feel.

Some of you *know* you're part of the family of God, but you don't *feel* part of it. Maybe you're a member of a local church but see a wide gap between what the body of Christ should be and what your experience of it has been. Maybe you're skeptical or withholding full-fledged participation due to some "rational ground for disappointment," as the demon Screwtape puts it in C. S. Lewis's *The Screwtape Letters*.[4] And perhaps that "rational ground" is legitimate. Or maybe it's not.

Churches are full of sinners still being sanctified, so each one will provide a "rational ground for disappointment" in some way. While you may choose to leave one local church to join another, don't quit the church completely. Don't quit fellowship with a local body of believers (and don't think that simply attending church online substitutes for what the New Testament calls church). Instead, look for a healthy church, one that "increasingly reflects God's character as his character has been revealed in his Word."[5]

You need the local church in order to flourish in the Christian life. Once you commit to a local church, take initiative. As our church's Local Disciple-Making Pastor likes to say: "Be a go-to person, not a come-to person."[6] If you want to be known, don't wait around for people to introduce themselves or invite you to sit with them. Be proactive. Introduce yourself and invite someone to sit with *you*. Join that church's equivalent of a small group and serve in the church. Don't wait to be on the receiving end of the "one anothers" before you begin practicing them yourself. If you feel like you don't have a place in the church or that no one in your local church knows you, how can *you* take a step to undo any unbelonging you may feel? You're an integral part of the body of Christ, even if you don't feel like it. Your presence and participation matters, not only for you, for you have something to contribute as well.

False Teaching Addressed in I John I

On top of being all-in with God's people, John shows us another way God heals our brokenness—by calling us to *truth* instead of lies, *change* instead of complacency, and *love* instead of apathy. How does John do this? By providing a three-prong test by which believers can evaluate themselves: a doctrine test, an obedience test, and a love test.[7] Do we believe truth about Jesus, as stated by Him and the apostles (doctrine test)? Is our behavior changing as we follow Jesus and His teachings (obedience test), and do our lives exemplify the love of Jesus (love test)? If so, there's no way our brokenness is staying as-is.

Verses 5–10 contain three "if we say" statements that help us understand some of the false teachings that prompted John to write the letter. We behave how we believe, and these false teachings led to false beliefs and false actions among John's original readers.

> If we say, "We have fellowship with him," and yet we walk in darkness, we are lying and are not practicing the truth. (v. 6)

> If we say, "We have no sin," we are deceiving ourselves, and the truth is not in us. (v. 8)

> If we say, "We have not sinned," we make him a liar, and his word is not in us. (v. 10)

Truth Instead of Lies

Let's start with "truth instead of lies," for this is one vital way God helps heal our brokenness. In chapter 1, John confronts the lie that you can become a Christian and not change. "God is light" is shorthand for God being pure, righteous, sinless, just, and holy (v. 5). No darkness—no sinfulness—exists in Him. To be in fellowship with light necessitates being in the light yourself, for darkness and light are incompatible. You can't walk in the light and the dark at the same time.

Living in sin equals living in darkness, so if you say you're a Christian but are habitually viewing porn, masturbating, reading/watching smutty content, shagging guys, engaging in homosexual behaviors, living with your boyfriend, cutting, cheating, getting drunk, shooting up, gossiping, lying, or stirring up drama (among other things)—you need to check yourself because you're walking in darkness, not light! You might say you're God's child, but your actions proclaim that you're far from Him. According to 1 John 1:6's standard, do you have fellowship with God?

If you think you can become a Christian and not change, you're believing and living some really bad doctrine. John is *not* saying you become a Christian by works. He's demonstrating that if your life doesn't match what you say you believe, then you don't really believe it. You have an unbelief issue. Your results from 1 John's obedience test demonstrate what you *actually* believe.

Change Instead of Complacency

Your brokenness won't heal if you believe lies instead of the truth and live in darkness instead of the light. Now, this takes time and doesn't occur overnight. Furthermore, walking in the light doesn't mean you'll live a sinless life. Instead, it means you won't try to excuse your sin, minimize it, explain it away, or blame it on others. It means acknowledging your sin to God, not attempting to hide from Him like Adam and Eve. It means confessing what you have done and turning from it. It's choosing to obey moment-by-moment, day-by-day. As Martin Luther explains:

> This life, therefore, is not righteousness but growth in righteousness, not health but

healing, not being but becoming, not rest but exercise. We are not yet what we shall be, but we are growing toward it. The process is not yet finished but it is what is going on. This is not the end but it is the road. All does not yet gleam in glory but all is being purified.[8]

During my senior year of college, a friend of mine died in a tragic accident. She wasn't a Christian, and her death left me with a lot of grief and guilt because I knew I'd missed opportunities to share the gospel with her. As I processed this loss, I began thinking about how I would spend my life, and I came across Jonathan Edwards' "Resolutions" where he declares: "Resolved, that I will live so, as I shall wish I had done when I come to die."[9]

When it's my time to die, I want to look back at my life without regret, which will only happen if I faithfully follow the Lord. A lifetime trajectory of faithfulness consists of daily faithfulness, being faithful today then tomorrow getting up and doing the same. Are you wasting your life, or are you stewarding it for the sake of God's glory and the advancement of His Kingdom?

With all of this, you may think you have nothing to contribute because of your story. I've talked with many young women who want to serve God as missionaries but whose churches or various sending agencies have made them feel "unsendable" because of their sin struggles, because they've experienced trauma, or because they have anxiety or depression. Do we need people to be in a good place with coping mechanisms, triggers, and medications before placing them in the stress of a cross-cultural ministry situation? Yes. But do these aspects of a person's story make them unusable to God? No!

You have a place in God's story no matter what your story entails. Ephesians 2:10 informs us that we are God's workmanship, "created in Christ Jesus for good works, which God prepared ahead of time for us to do." Paul writes this about *all*

Christians. He doesn't specify that it's only for the Christians who haven't been abused, dealt with addiction, or struggled with sexual sin. He's got a place for you in His work and His story. Nothing about your story is wasted in God's economy. You may think it's too late or that you've wasted too much of your life already. But that's not the case! That sort of thinking disbelieves the gospel and puts a cap on God's grace and sovereignty.

Friend, you do not have the one stronghold God cannot defeat. You do not have the one life that does not matter. You do not have the one story God cannot use.

Love Instead of Apathy

While believing truth, walking in the light, and pursuing obedience are all part of the Christian life and how God heals our brokenness, there's one final part that John highlights in his letter—love. As we grow in Christ, the fruit of love increasingly shows itself in our interactions with others, and John ties this love of others back to our understanding of the love of God.

One of my prayers in writing this book is that I would make God attractive to you by presenting Him as He is. It's so easy to write about sin and present a list of do's and don'ts for the sinner. The how-tos of fighting sin are helpful, but you miss the point of obedience if you lack love for the One you're obeying or if you don't grasp His love for you. The beauty of God's heart for you shows itself in sending His Son to die, taking the punishment for your sin and mine (1 John 4:8–11). However, it's easy for familiarity with this truth to lead us to no longer marvel at it.

But here's what's true about God's love for you: God's heart is to move toward you, not away from you. Compassion and patience is His knee-jerk response to you, not frustration and impatience. He knows your failures, but because of Christ, He doesn't hold them against you. He understands you and your struggles better than you do, and He's tender toward you and gentle with you.[10] He makes Himself available and accessible to you 24/7. Even though He's God of the universe, He's not too busy for you. Your cares and concerns are not too small or trite for Him; in fact, He *invites* you to bring your burdens to Him.[11]

You won't experience God's transformation of your brokenness without grasping His love and letting the truth of it transform you. His love provides motivation and hope as we continue our fight against sin. It also prompts us to live in the light, for as scary as the light can be, His love moves us toward change rather than continuing in complacency with the darkness.

Freedom in I John

After engaging in porn and masturbation for about a decade, Darcy confessed her sin to her mentor and started counseling, but as much as Darcy hates her sin and how she feels when she acts out, her attempts at sobriety have resulted in one failure after another. As Darcy and I talked about the guilt and shame she feels, she relayed that these feelings have made it hard to connect with God as well as with fellow Christians. But her mentor has provided a beautiful contradiction to her feelings, for no matter how many times Darcy has come to her confessing her failure once again, her mentor has responded with patience, compassion, and care. Darcy noted how this mentor's responses have not only shown her love; they've also helped her to better understand *God's* love. For if her mentor—another human—could be this patient and loving toward her, *how much more* is God patient and loving toward her?

We know at this point that God gives us a spiritual family, and in this community, we support one another in following Christ and in telling others about Him. Whether our hurts come from our suffering or from sinful choices, our healing journey does not occur in isolation. In verse 7, John hinges our fellowship with one another on walking in the light, and Darcy's story is one example of how walking in the light with her small group leader has led to greater fellowship but how it's also being used to combat guilt and shame and to remind her of how God sees her. It's helping her fight lies with truth. Darcy is still in process, but she's recognized that she doesn't have to have her act together before being in fellowship with other Christians. Rather, she *needs* that fellowship to help her continue fighting against sin!

Like Darcy, you may continue to stumble as you battle temptation, so what helps us get back on the path after we stumble? Let's see what 1 John 1:7–9 has to say:

> If we walk in the light as he himself is in the light, we have fellowship with one another, and the blood of Jesus his Son cleanses us from all sin. If we say, "We have no sin," we are deceiving ourselves, and the truth is not in us. If we confess our sins, he is faithful and righteous to forgive us our sins and to cleanse us from all unrighteousness.

In addition to fellowship hinging on walking in the light, verse 7 also bases our experience of Christ's cleansing on walking in the light. We cannot have freedom from sin if we do not confess it, for freedom from sin only comes from walking in the light about our sin.

Let's talk a minute about what confession actually is. It involves acknowledging what we've done. We bring what we've done to light, rather than letting it hide in the darkness. Some of the original recipients of John's letter lived in denial of their sin (v. 8). They weren't acknowledging their sinfulness, but we can't get free of what we refuse to see. We must face our sin and acknowledge it to God.

I love how verse 7 says Jesus cleanses us from *all* sin. Not just some of it, but *all* of it. Does this mean we won't experience consequences for our sins? No. God's forgiveness doesn't absolve us of consequences in this life, but it does for the life to come.

Jesus' blood purifies those who confess their sins, and the verb tense used here suggests this is an activity that was completed in the past with implications for the present. What does this mean? It means that the sins you currently commit are *already* paid for in the past by Christ. *And* you can experience God's cleansing power in real time for those sins when you bring them into the light. As often as we sin, we should confess that sin to God.

So let's say you do this. You confess your sin. Now what? Something called *repentance* is the next step. Repentance means *change*. You turn away from what you were doing, and instead of doing *that*, you obey Christ. We can confess sin without any intention of repentance, but that's not the type of confession 1 John 1:9 promotes. Actually, it's not true confession at all. Jesus' cleansing blood is not a cover-up for someone who wants to keep sinning. It's the help a person needs who truly wants to change.

This lifestyle of confessing and repenting is how we walk in the light. This is what it looks like to cooperate with God in this "already-not yet" journey of healing your brokenness. Let me explain what I mean by your healing being "already-not yet." When we become a Christian, we're saved from the penalty of sin, and we have the promise of complete healing and restoration in the life to come.[12] This promise is so dependable— so sure—we can speak of "already" having it. But at the same time, our daily reality shows that our brokenness has "not yet" been healed. We continue to sin in this life. We continue to process our pain. We continue to deal with the effects of trauma and other hurts we've experienced. When we become Christians, God makes us new, but we're not yet perfected. Our journey of healing won't be complete until we're reunited with Christ in the life to come. But that time of complete healing *will* come for all who follow Christ.

This past week, I heard quite a few confessions from young women that included: getting pregnant outside of marriage, cutting, smoking weed, underage drinking, taking a Plan B pill, viewing lesbian porn, hatred, and masturbating. A lot of bringing things to light happened this week, and each confession presented an opportunity to remind these young women about God's forgiveness and how God sees them because of Christ.

What a week to be writing on 1 John, which proclaims Christ's faithfulness to forgive us our sins and to cleanse us from "all" unrighteousness (1 John 1:9)! What a week to be meditating on Jesus Christ being our Advocate before the Father and the atoning sacrifice for our sins (1 John 2:1–2)! What a week to be reminded that—no matter what we've done—we can be made clean by God and have a right relationship with Him (1 John 1:5–8)! What a week to be reminded of the community He has created with fellowship predicated on living honestly (1 John 1:3–8)!

Dear one, Jesus is not intimidated by your life. You are not "too much" for Him. He's not daunted by your past or your present. You do not have the one story He cannot redeem. In fact, He's already defeated your sin—including your "worst" ones—on the cross. Not only that, but the place of your greatest shame and guilt is known and covered by your Savior. That place of deepest wounding—He knows you there, and He loves you there.

Walking in the light doesn't mean perfection, but it does mean you're in the process of becoming more like Him. You can't successfully fight against sin with your own willpower and strength. Neither can you do it alone. The fellowship of God's people—all of us sinners saved by God's grace—provides companions for the journey. By God's design, we don't have to be in the trenches alone.

Who knows the real you? What next step do you need to take to walk in the light? Who will you invite to walk alongside you as you fight against sin? How can you support fellow sisters in the trenches? In doing these things, we are working with God as He moves to heal our brokenness, and we will be the body of Christ God intended us to be.

> Through many dangers, toils, and snares
> I have already come;
> 'Tis grace hath brought me safe thus far,
> and grace will lead me home.[13]

>> **APPENDIX A** <<

A Tool for Discerning If a Sexual Act Is Sinful

IN THE ACCOMPANYING CHART, THE SIX CHARACTERISTICS OF God's design for sex (heterosexual, relational, covenantal, fruitful, selfless, and symbolic) are listed at the top of each column. The column farthest to the left includes various sexual acts that have been discussed in the book. While it's not an all-encompassing list, it shows how the framework operates.

For an act to *not* be considered a sexual sin, it must uphold *each and every one* of these six characteristics of God's design for sex. For example, homosexuality is not **heterosexual**, so that box remains empty. Because it occurs with another human being, it *is* **relational**, so it checks that box. Depending on where you live in the world is whether or not homosexual couples can get married, but while a homosexual person may legally marry in the U.S., we do not depend on culture's definition of marriage as a covenantal relationship. We rely on God's definition of marriage, which is between one man and one woman; therefore, I do *not* put homosexuality as checking the box of the **covenantal** category.

It might be argued that homosexual sex can strengthen a relationship; but at the same time, it can never produce children (not because of infertility or suffering due to the Fall but because, anatomically, it is out of alignment with the way two heterosexual bodies can procreate). As a result, the **fruitful** category should remain either unchecked or with a question mark. As for the **selfless** category, because sex falls under common grace, both heterosexual and homosexual people can strive to be honoring instead of selfish with their partner, although this isn't always the case. With this in mind, I put a question mark in the corresponding box.

Lastly, homosexuality does not accurately reflect Christ's relationship with the church, for it depicts a relationship where sameness replaces complementarity. Instead of Christ and the church, it depicts two of the same: Christ and Christ or the church and the church. For God, the spiritual reality came first with earthly marriage pointing to it, so the **symbolic** category remains empty. Although homosexuality checks 1½ of the six categories, it does not satisfy all six of them, which demonstrates that homosexuality does *not* align with God's design for sex and is, therefore, a sin.

I have filled in the rest of the table, and you'll notice several question marks on it. These represent where something could *possibly* fit that category. For example, sexual fantasies, sex dolls, pornography, erotica, AV/VR relationships and sex, and sexual violence can all be heterosexual, but they can also be homosexual, which is why I put a question mark for those acts in the heterosexual column. BDSM and sexual violence can occur within the marriage covenant, but couples who are not married can also practice BDSM or violate their partner, which is why I put a question mark in that column.

I intentionally gave you a couple of blank sections at the end of the table in case there are other sexual acts you want to add to the table, so you can work the framework and determine if the act aligns with God's design for sex. Keep in mind that for an act to be permissible, *it must check off each box with an "✓," not a question mark.*

Formulas and frameworks make it easy to become legalistic, so please understand that my intent is for you to see at a glance all that has been discussed with regard to the six aspects of God's design for sex. I pray that the visual helps you to remember truths about His design and to connect the dots on why certain sexual acts are sin. Knowing God's truth enables us to identify when something goes against His design, and I desire for you to be grounded in His truth and confident in His goodness.

Six Aspects of God's Design for Sex

	Heterosexual	Relational	Covenantal	Fruitful	Selfless	Symbolic
AR/VR Relationships and Sex	?					
BDSM	?	✓	?			
Erotica	?					
Fantasy (not about your spouse)	?					
Homosexuality		✓			?	
Masturbation						
Polyamorous Relationships	?	✓	?	?	?	
Polygamy	?	✓	✓	✓	?	
Pornography	?	✓		✓		
Premarital or Extramarital Sex	?	✓		✓	?	
Sex Dolls or Sexbots	?					
Sexual Violence	?	✓	?	?		

» APPENDIX B «

A Word on Sex Addiction

WHEN DOES A SEXUAL STRUGGLE GO FROM BEING A STRUGGLE to an addiction? I found myself asking this very question while discipling women who were battling sexual sin. Because sex addiction is complex and requires more than a chapter to adequately address it, this appendix won't give you all the answers, but as I share what I've learned from the trenches, it will get you started, beginning with the fact that there's more than one type of sex addiction.

I don't know what image comes to mind when you think of a sex addict, but you probably won't recognize a sex addict when you meet one. While you might picture a street-hardened prostitute or a scantily clad woman, the female sex addicts I know dress like your average student, businesswoman, or church member. Also, virgins can be sex addicts, and addicts are represented in every ethnic group, socioeconomic status, religion, age, marital status, family background, and gender.

Pornography might be the category of sex addiction you're most familiar with, but sex addiction also includes **masturbation**, **fantasy**, and **exhibitionism**. **Romance addicts** like the chase but drop the object of their attention as soon as they've hooked them. The high comes from the seduction, from falling in love, and from pursuing or being pursued by a person, and this addict may or may not engage in intercourse.

Another common form of sex addiction is **sex and love addiction**. To clarify, the relationships can involve sex or be emotionally dependent and not involve sex.[1] The emphasis here is on the codependent nature of the addict. The sex and love addict confuses manipulation, control, and neediness with love, enmeshing with the partner and fearing abandonment by them. These relationships can be heterosexual or homosexual, and the person can have one relationship or be juggling more than one at a time.

All of these behaviors fall under the umbrella term of sex addiction, and this list is not exhaustive. Take any of the sexual sins discussed in this book, and they can be turned into an addiction. But how do you discern if the sin struggle has escalated to a sexual addiction?

You Might Be an Addict If . . .

If you're wondering whether you or someone you love is a sex addict, consider the following questions:

Are you OBSESSED with the behavior? Does it preoccupy your thoughts? Does the preoccupation interfere with daily life? Do you find yourself spacing out during conversations because you're obsessing or daydreaming about acting out? Are you missing out on living life because you're either thinking about acting out or engaging in the act? Do hours, days, or even weeks go by where you barely remember what you did because you were thinking about acting out and/or doing it? Are you consumed with the object of your obsession?

Is the behavior COMPULSIVE? Once you begin thinking about the behavior, does it feel impossible to *not* act out? Do you feel like once you start, you can't stop? Do you feel driven or compelled to engage in the behavior, even if you'd previously determined not to do it? Do you find yourself acting out, even when you don't want to? Do you feel like some overwhelming force within you just takes over?

Do you use the behavior as a means to COPE? Why are you engaging in the behavior? What are you trying to achieve? Is it an anesthetic for emotional pain? A way to forget trauma? Is it for personal satisfaction or a sense of power? Emotions serve as powerful triggers, and for the sex addicts I have known, they act out to cope with boredom, loneliness, anger, anxiety, sadness, stress, resentment, and shame. While initially the behavior serves the addict, providing the desired results, the addict eventually serves the addiction, becoming dominated by it. The behavior betrays them in the end, and instead of alleviating problems, it causes more.

Do you have SPECIAL ROUTINES associated with acting out? Having considered acting out, are there things you begin to do to prepare for it? Maybe it's finding a private place or planning the time you know everyone at home will be asleep. Maybe it's accessing your smartphone, laptop, a sexually graphic novel, or Netflix. Maybe it's driving by a particular place on your way home from work. Maybe it's dressing a particular way before hitting the club, looking for your next potential sexual liaison. Some ritualistic behaviors take only a few minutes; others may involve more time because of grooming potential partners. Another way to think about ritualization is to consider what your MO is with acting out. The addict may not be aware of their ritual, but participating in these special routines builds anticipation and excitement as the addict continues to obsess about their addictive behavior.

Has your behavior become UNMANAGEABLE? Have you experienced failure in your attempts to stop? Have you felt unable to *stay* stopped? Do you feel out of control and powerless to stop, despite your intentions and best efforts? Do you set boundaries only to find that you're never able to keep them? Whenever you set a line or boundary, do you find yourself moving past it, never stopping when you say you will?

Do you feel like you live a DOUBLE LIFE? Do you feel like two different people? There's the exterior that others see at work, church, school, or home; then there's the you that you know. The you who goes places considered immoral or shameful. The you who does things you wouldn't want anyone to know about. The you who engages with people in unhealthy, sinful ways. You may even feel appalled at yourself and struggle to believe what you have done.

Do you continue acting out despite NEGATIVE CONSEQUENCES? The adverse consequences could be health related (STDs, sexual violence, unwanted pregnancy, etc.) or could involve legal consequences. Or maybe you have been discovered and despite promises made or threats of losing a job or relationship, you continue in the behavior. Or maybe acting out has consumed so much of your time and attention that you've lost friendships, made poor grades, struggled financially, or caught flak at work because of your poor job performance. Acting out also levies an emotional toll on the individual, for addicts feel shame, despair, and self-loathing as a result of the cycle they find themselves in. Engaging in sin also affects the person spiritually, for sin hinders our fellowship with God. While God offers forgiveness, engaging in habitual sin demonstrates our lack of repentance and the depth of our idolatry, and His grace does *not* give us license to continue in sin.

Have you noticed an ESCALATION in the frequency, duration, or types of behavior in which you've engaged? Has your behavior gotten progressively worse? Maybe you started with soft porn, but then it escalated to something more novel, more violent, or even illegal. Maybe acting out has jumped from porn to people, leading you to massage parlors, prostitutes, or one-night stands. Just as a person's tolerance increases with alcohol or drugs, sexual activity affects a person neurologically, causing their tolerance to increase to where they need more time or novelty to get the same "high" as before.

Do you currently have or have you ever had another ADDICTION? I have seen many young women quit one addiction only to start another. Trading one addiction for another demonstrates that the issues prompting the addictive behavior have not been dealt with. The person has simply transferred their method of coping from one behavior to another. It's also common for an individual to begin a second addiction in order to cope with the first.[2] They may act out sexually in order to cope with the shame or isolation associated with their alcoholism or drug addiction.

Do you experience an EMOTIONAL CRASH after acting out? Despair oozes when you *again* do that which you promised yourself (and others) you wouldn't do. Self-contempt results when *you* can't believe what you've done. Anguish emanates from the high not being as great or lasting as long as you desired. Hopelessness ensues when you question whether or not change is actually possible. Your actions reinforce the shame you've experienced. You felt worthless, unlovable, evil, dirty, etc. before acting out, but now, those things feel even *truer*. Instead of being a deterrent, such feelings prompt you to consider acting out again as a way to numb the pain. Or maybe you question what's the point of trying when you'll eventually give in anyway. In this emotional crash, suicide often presents itself as an exit strategy for all your problems. Some people do penance in order to anesthetize themselves or make themselves "more acceptable" to God, doing good deeds or throwing themselves into Bible study or Scripture memorization. Others punish themselves, sometimes even literally with various forms of self-flagellation. But none of these behaviors mask how you feel about yourself.

While the questions above are not an official diagnostic assessment, they do provide an informal way to delineate between a struggle with sexual sin and an addiction to it. Patrick Carnes defines an addict as one who "has a pathological relationship with a mood-altering chemical."[3] Thinking about alcoholism or drug addiction, this makes sense. The person uses the chemical to alter their mood and develops a destructive relationship with the chemical, becoming dependent on it. Sex addiction replaces that chemical with a behavior or experience, which also affects our hormones and neurotransmitters.

On a neurochemical level, sexual activity affects the brain identically to how crack cocaine affects it.[4] This is why it's *not* helpful to tell an addict to just "stop it." Before addiction, a person has a baseline in the brain regarding dopamine and sex, but addiction distorts that baseline. Recovery involves resetting the baseline, which is an arduous, time-consuming process. But these changes to the brain are reversible, for God has given our brain (like our muscles) a use-it-or-lose-it function.

The neurological component of addiction is one factor to consider, but acting out is also a choice, a sinful choice that reflects what a person worships. Counselor Edward Welch defines addiction as "a bondage to the rule of a substance, activity, or state of mind, which then becomes the center of life, defending itself from the truth so that even bad consequences don't bring repentance, and leading to further estrangement from God."[5]

With this understanding, a person becomes enslaved to their addictive behavior, and it becomes the object of their worship. Addiction = slavery, and the slavery stems from idolatry. In responding to sin, including sin that's become an addiction, we must deal with the disordered worship in our own lives.

How to Break Free of Sexual Addiction

For the struggler, fighting against ingrained behaviors means confronting hard truths about yourself, learning new coping skills, and living honestly with God, yourself, and others. As you contemplate pursuing sobriety, consider Israel's journey from slavery to freedom in Exodus.

When God sent Moses and Aaron to confront Pharaoh about releasing God's people from slavery, Pharaoh made life harder for the Israelites while still requiring them to meet their previous work quotas. By oppressing them, Pharaoh intended to demoralize the people, and it worked.

Ultimately, we cannot release ourselves from the slavery of addiction. We need the Lord to deliver us from the slavery we've placed ourselves in. But if you, like the Israelites, expect deliverance to occur swiftly and easily, your expectations will result in premeditated resentment. God can deliver you from your addiction, but will you trust Him, even on the days when a step of obedience seems to make everything feel worse instead of better?

In Exodus 5:22–23, how did Moses respond to Pharaoh's increased oppression? He sought the Lord who reminded him that He doesn't forget His promises, isn't ignorant of His people's suffering, and that He has a plan (Exod. 6:4–13). His plan entailed sending ten plagues to judge Egypt over the course of one to two years (Exod. 6–12), and during this time, Israel waited for freedom, daily choosing whether they'd obey God. Their freedom wasn't immediate, but their obedience was supposed to be.

The Israelites' faith wasn't perfect, but God responded to their mustard seed-sized faith. With each plague, Israel saw another miracle, and it built their trust in Him. This generation of Israelites had never experienced freedom, and after four hundred years of slavery, they'd become forlorn. Through the plagues, God taught them to hope in *Him*. They could anticipate their final deliverance with each step toward freedom. They could trust He'd bring His promises to pass, even if they didn't live to see their fulfillment.

After the Passover in Exodus 12, God didn't lead Israel to the Promised Land using the most direct path—but with good reason: "When Pharaoh let the people go, God did not lead them along the road to the land of the Philistines, even though it was nearby; for God said, 'The people will change their minds and return to Egypt if they face war.'"[6] God knew Israel wasn't ready for the combat required by the most direct path. There were some challenges they would fail if faced at that particular time, so He led them out of Egypt toward the Red Sea and the Sinai Peninsula.

Your freedom is not just about you; it's also about the glory of God's name. You have many enemies that need to be defeated—your pride, your view of reality, your self-loathing, and your shame. God's plan considers all the facets of your situation, the lives of others, His glory, and the advancement of the gospel, so while the path He lays out for you may not always make sense to you, every aspect of His plan has purpose.

The same God who called Israel out of slavery went ahead of His people, leading them to freedom. When Pharaoh and his military chased Israel to the Red Sea, Israel cried to the Lord for help. God fought for His people and showed Himself greater than Israel's enemies by decimating Pharaoh's *entire* army and enabling Israel to cross the Red Sea on *dry* ground, freeing them from slavery.

I don't know where you are in your relationship with God, but if you want out of your slavery to sin, God is the only One who can break the chains of your bondage and set you free. Are you willing to turn from your sin? Will you submit to God and trust Him? This will involve a daily commitment and a daily ordering of yourself under His authority. Praise Him, we *can* experience victory over sin in this life because He has conquered sin once and for all, and if you are a Christian, the same One who conquered sin lives *in* you.

Address the Physical and Behavioral

Breaking free from sex addiction requires consideration of the *whole* person. This entails addressing the behavioral aspect of sin as well as motivations for the behavior. As you pursue sobriety, you will need relational support, so this aspect of your life will require attention. Lastly, all sin must be understood in light of who God is, and because all sin is a worship issue, you must reckon with who or what it is you're worshiping and whether you're willing to forsake sin and follow God.

God graciously made the brain to be adaptable, possessing a use-it-or-lose-it function,[7] but to reset the brain's baseline with regard to dopamine levels, abstinence will be necessary. Sexual activity of any kind interferes with the brain's process of lowering the tolerance threshold. Commit to ninety days of abstinence from all sexual activity in order to allow time for your brain to detox,[8] and if you have any rituals associated with your acting out, identify and abstain from them as well. This allows the brain to reset in how it responds to sexual behavior, and it also provides evidence to refute the lie that sex is a need and that the addictive behavior is required.

For the person who is married, this entails communication and support from your spouse (1 Cor. 7:5). While your partner may initially resist this decision, explain that long-term sobriety requires a short-term sexual time-out, for your brain must begin to reverse the neurological effects of such ingrained behavior. Because of how sex has been utilized by one or both spouses within marriage, many issues in the marriage will likely manifest during this period of abstinence, and it would be wise to seek counseling for what all will come up in the pursuit of sobriety.

To clarify, sex isn't sinful *when it's engaged in according to God's design*, which means that it's heterosexual, relational, covenantal, fruitful, selfless, and symbolic. Any behavior that is sinful should continue being abstained from *after* the ninety-day period. But, for example, intercourse is not sinful for a married couple; therefore, they should resume marital relations after the abstinence period. In this way, sex addiction differs from alcohol or drug addiction. For the married person struggling with sex addiction, they have to learn how to engage in healthy sexuality with their spouse without resorting to their acting out patterns.

During the abstinence period, you will likely experience withdrawals while the body adjusts and the brain resets, and withdrawals may last days or weeks. Symptoms can include irritability, mood swings, fatigue, insomnia, anxiety, difficulty concentrating, depression, rapid heartbeat, headaches, increased appetite, itchy skin, and nausea.[9] These symptoms do subside, but if you have questions or cause for concern, please see a medical professional.

As you pursue sobriety, expect temptation or cravings. Physically and emotionally, you will be weak and vulnerable, especially in the early days of recovery. Within her first three months of sobriety, one young woman called me to explain how she couldn't even leave the house and drive to her Bible study group because temptation was so strong that, if she got in the car, she knew she'd end up acting out instead of going to Bible study. At that moment, resisting temptation meant staying home and not even getting in the car.

For friends and family, you will feel helpless as you watch someone go through all of this. Continue to encourage and pray for them, especially during the initial ninety-day abstinence period. This will *not* be the time to reason with them or delve into their underlying root issues. Let the person stabilize physically. During the abstinence period, the brain is rewiring and making new connections, which means that simply refraining from their ingrained behavior patterns will require expansive amounts of energy. During this time, the person needs your compassion, encouragement, prayers, and listening ear—not your lectures, information, or pent-up frustration.

Create a Plan

Identify triggers and create a plan for avoiding them and for resisting temptation when it hits. What can you do instead of acting out? Think ahead and write out your options, putting them on your phone or a sticky note for quick reference. As discussed in chapter 11, seek the things that are above, set your mind on things above, put sin to death, and put on the traits listed in Colossians 3.

If your plan involves calling or spending time with friends or family, discuss with them what is needed. Have a code word (like SOS) that signals to them that this is a sobriety call, not a catch-up call, so they can know to respond quickly. Include more than one person in your plan, in case someone isn't available when you reach out.

This will be a season of resisting temptation and learning new coping skills, but by God's grace and strength, you *can* move forward in recovery. He wants us to obey Him, but this doesn't mean obedience is easy.

A Word on Relapse

As an imperfect human, you will struggle, and you might even relapse, delving back into old habits of sexual sin, but progress can be made even in the midst of failure.

Consider your favorite maps app on your smartphone. If you type in a destination and take one wrong turn, it reroutes you, so you're still headed toward the correct final destination. If you take a wrong turn in your pursuit of sobriety, will you choose to pick back up and go in the right direction, or will you ignore the GPS and keep making wrong turns? If you sin, repent and continue on the trajectory of obedience. Don't let one wrong turn devolve into a trajectory of sin.

I count it as progress when girls quickly reach out to confess instead of waiting days or weeks during which they continue to sin. It's progress when they voluntarily tell me versus waiting for me to check in. It's progress when they go from hooking up with guys on a regular basis to being concerned about their flirtatious behavior with men. It's progress when they respond to work stress by calling a friend when they get home rather than viewing porn. Be encouraged by any and all steps taken toward God. Even baby steps are steps. If you are walking alongside someone as they fight against sexual sin, point out these things to them, for they are indicators of God working in them.

Obedience occurs one step at a time and one day at a time. You won't perfectly obey God on this earth because you're not perfect, but you can engage in a *trajectory* of obedience by His grace.

Address the Emotional

Abstinence does not solve the problem of addiction, for sobriety requires facing the beliefs and emotions you were self-medicating to cover up. Rather than acting out to numb or ignore, we should experience the emotions, name them, examine them, and learn to deal with them in God-honoring ways. In taking away addictive coping strategies, emotions *will* rise to the surface. Dealing with your sin necessitates dealing honestly with yourself.

As part of your sobriety journey, write out a detailed account of your sexual history and addictive behaviors. Describe what you have done, who you have hurt along the way, and how your choices have affected all areas of your life. What was your motivation for acting out? What end result were you wanting? How did you deceive others or yourself in order to act out? How have you been selfish and self-consumed? Clarify what your actions express about your views of God, yourself, and others.

In writing your history, you will be tempted to blame-shift, cover up, or present yourself in a positive light. Instead, acknowledge what *you* have done. Take responsibility for *your* actions. Self-deception, manipulation, hiding, and rationalization enabled you to continue your sinful habits; breaking that cycle requires honesty and bringing *all* of your sin to light. If it's helpful, use the webbing tool from chapter 11 to process, and after writing out your personal inventory, courageously read it to a trusted friend, mentor, counselor, or support group.

This work of pursuing emotional health will begin during the ninety-day abstinence period, but it will continue long afterward. When you feel tempted to act out, examine why. What about your situation prompts you to feel that acting out is the best solution?

As you go through life, different seasons—particularly ones that are stressful or involve change—may trigger temptation. Although challenging, these seasons can reveal facets of our lives that still need to be sanctified. Remember, sanctification is a lifelong process, and God is at work to conform us to the image of His Son for our good and for our joy.

Address the Relational

Make Amends

While sin destroys relationships, following God transforms them. Your pursuit of sin has affected others, and obedience to God involves making amends to those you've hurt.

To begin, use the personal inventory you've written to identify all who have been affected by your sin.[10] The list may include the people in the porn you've viewed, past sexual partners, people you have deceived or manipulated, the individuals you have fantasized about, or those you have neglected or resented. Create an initial list, knowing you'll likely be adding to it as you remember the past.

Unless doing so would injure someone, go in sincerity and humility to these individuals, admit how you have wronged them, and ask for their forgiveness. This will take some time to do and won't be easy. Use wisdom in what you share, considering the best interest of the other person, and seek counsel as you do this. Many will want to see change from you more than hear your apology, but making amends is a helpful starting point to build on. People may or may not forgive you, or they may forgive you but not want to reconcile with you, which is their choice. You cannot control this, but you can be faithful in what God asks of *you*.

Build a Support System of Fellow Christians

Who are the people who can support you as you fight against sin? You may read this and realize you have no such people or that you've driven them all away. Ask God to provide trustworthy believers in your life and take steps to engage in community. Put yourself in places where you can meet other Christians and take initiative to get to know people, asking them about themselves. It takes time to build friendships, but you need a support system to help you fight sin.

Not only do you need people, you specifically need *the church*. Recovery groups are wonderful gifts, but they do not substitute for the body of Christ. Non-believers cannot minister to you in the same way that brothers and sisters in Christ can, for believers can point you to gospel truth, call out idolatry, and remind you of who you are in Christ.

While active participation in a local church is vital for a Christian's spiritual health, the people there may or may not know how to respond to your experiences. The church is full of imperfect people, but that is no excuse for sequestering from it. It may take time to find a solid local church (if you haven't already) and to identify believers there with whom you can share your story. It will be easy to tell yourself that no one will accept you or that the church is full of hypocrites. The people there may not know what it's like to be you, but they do know what it's like to be tempted, to fail, and to need grace.

For the alongsiders, you may not know what to do, but you can listen. You can also pray, remind the person of God's truth, and read and listen to podcasts in order to learn more about sex addiction and sexual sin. Furthermore, people who are coming out of the mire of sexual sin and addiction will be emotionally immature. They will not know how to relate in healthy ways, and it will be a process to learn new ways of relating that don't involve manipulation, control, and deceit. Your friendship can model what healthy relating looks like and provide a place for them to practice being honest, caring for others, and sharing their feelings.

Those in recovery need you to seek them out when they've gone radio silent and to not let them fall through the cracks. Celebrate sobriety anniversaries with them. If there are dates on the calendar that are triggering for them, be aware and surround them with community at such times. A sex addict recently relayed to me how her recovery group helped her get sober but her church helped her heal because of the community she found there. I pray this will be true of the church at large—that we would be known as a place that welcomes sinners, walks with them, and helps them find true healing in Christ.

Utilize Community Resources

If your community offers recovery groups, I encourage you to participate in them. Celebrate Recovery is a Christ-centered 12-step group for people struggling with a range of things (celebraterecovery.com), and Sex Addicts Anonymous (SAA) and Sex and Love Addicts Anonymous (SLAA) are 12-step groups specifically for people who struggle with sex addiction. Know that SAA and SLAA groups do not acknowledge God as the "Higher Power" and, instead, allow individuals to define their own higher power. These groups allow each individual to self-identify their problematic behaviors and do not call sin "sin," so know this going in if you read their curriculum or join such groups. Not every community has a Christian recovery group or even an SAA or SLAA group, but there are SAA and SLAA groups where you can phone in or join digitally.

Twelve-step groups provide structure and support for addicts. The people in these groups personally understand the struggle, and if you choose to get a sponsor, they essentially disciple you as you work through the program's steps. Recovery groups provide a network of "sober sisters" you can call if you find yourself in danger of acting out. Ideally, it would be wonderful to find such support in a local church, and if that is available to you, pursue it. But secular recovery groups can also equip you as you fight against sin.

Counselors are also resources. We see specialists when we have heart, brain, or lung problems, and the same principle should apply to our intrapersonal and interpersonal issues. When it comes to sex addiction, licensed therapists can become Certified Sexual Addiction Therapists (CSATs), meaning they're specifically trained to therapeutically address the behaviors, denial, trauma, partner(s), and legal issues of the counselee. A CSAT may not be available in your area, and if not, find a healthy clinician who has training in addiction and/or trauma. This information can be ascertained by reading the biography of the counselor on their website or by calling their office and asking if this is in their wheelhouse.

Address the Spiritual

Ultimately, we sin because of our desires (James 1:14), and those desires drive us to satisfy ourselves in some way. Our actions are directly guided by what we worship and want, so it follows that we must cultivate a greater desire for the Lord. We must "taste and see that the LORD is good" and take refuge in Him (Ps. 34:8). As we do this, we'll increasingly act in ways that align with that desire for Him. So increasing our spiritual desire for God helps push out our desire for other things, and as a result, our behavior moves from acting out in sin to acting in godliness.

There's a young woman in recovery I'm journeying alongside who recently noted how her desires are shifting, and it's directly related to her intake of God's Word. Over the past couple of months, she's become more consistent in reading Scripture, and she's tasting and seeing the Lord's goodness, recognizing that her addictive behaviors pale in comparison to God. Whereas sin is "an ever-increasing craving for an ever-diminishing pleasure,"[11] she's discovering that time with the Lord is an ever-increasing pleasure with depths that can never be fathomed.

Not only does Scripture show us God's goodness, it presents us with truth. When Jesus speaks of the vine and the branches in John 15, He notes that branches—people—who abide in Him bear "much fruit."[12] Deceit accompanies addiction, but when people begin growing their relationship with God, honesty is a fruit. They begin to tell the truth and tell it quickly, and they begin to recognize what is true about God, themselves, and their circumstances.

Sometimes, this can be a lot to bear, but you won't grasp how marvelous God's grace and mercy is without first acknowledging what a wretched sinner you are. You must recognize your sinfulness to see how the gospel applies to *you*.

Knowing that our hope "is built on nothing less than Jesus' blood and righteousness"[13] keeps us from delving into despair. *Christ* has the last word, not your sin or addiction. You may have become a slave to your cravings, but if you are a Christian, "thank God that, although you used to be slaves of sin, you obeyed from the heart that pattern of teaching to which you were handed over, and having been set free from sin, you became enslaved to righteousness."[14]

In light of these truths, will you turn to God and allow Him to transform your behavior, your emotions, and your relationships? Will you grow your relationship with Him, trusting that He is sweeter and more satisfying than any addiction?

>> APPENDIX C <<

A Word on Sexual Abuse

AS PART OF OUR CHURCH'S INITIATIVE TO CARE FOR SURVIVORS of abuse, I invited several young women to lunch at my house to offer feedback about what caring well looks like. Although they were not coming to share details about their abuse, attending meant bravely letting others know that abuse is part of their story. I sat and listened for hours as these survivors relayed what has been helpful to them in their journey, how to respond well to an abuse disclosure, what they would like to hear taught by church leaders, and a whole slew of other topics.

Even though that conversation occurred months ago, I'm still ruminating on it. One of the ladies mentioned that it wasn't until she started counseling that she connected the dots between her abuse and her other struggles (sexual sin, eating disorder, mental health issues, relational patterns, etc.). This tracks with what I've seen with so many young women throughout my time in ministry, and it's why I'm addressing abuse in this book.

Many of you experienced abuse as a child or teen, others as an adult, and as a resourceful person, you've found ways to continue living while coping with what has been done to you. While not all of these coping mechanisms have been healthy, your continued functioning speaks to your creativity, courage, and determination. That you have endured something that is unendurable indicates that you can—by God's grace—face and heal from your abuse.

For some, your abuse launched you on a trajectory of coping that involved sexual sin, and your current trajectory would be different if the abuse had not occurred. You might never have struggled with this particular brand of sexual sin had you not been aroused or exposed to sexual activity through your abuse. Sin is still sin, so being sinned against doesn't make it okay to sin in response. But it does make how you got here understandable.

No matter what age you were when abused, what you were wearing, where you were, or who you were with—you were sinned against. You did not deserve what happened to you. It was wrong for someone to use you. You were *not* treated in accordance with your value as an image-bearer of the Almighty, and God hates what has been done to you.

What Is Abuse?

In *Domestic Abuse*, Darby Strickland helpfully describes abuse as "oppression," which acknowledges the behavior as a cruel and unjust expression of authority and emphasizes a pattern of controlling, coercive, and punishing actions.[1] The Bible, particularly Psalms, contains many references to oppression, some of which record the cries, questions, and petitions of those who were *currently* experiencing oppression:

> I will say to God, my rock, "Why have you forgotten me? Why must I go about in sorrow because of the enemy's **oppression**?" (Ps. 42:9)

> Wake up, LORD! Why are you sleeping? Get
> up! Don't reject us forever! Why do you hide
> and forget our affliction and **oppression**? (Ps.
> 44:23–24)

> May he [God] vindicate the afflicted among the
> people, help the poor, and crush the **oppres-
> sor**. (Ps. 72:4)

Scripture also records God's response to oppression:

> The LORD executes acts of righteousness and
> justice for all the **oppressed**. (Ps. 103:6)

> He remains faithful forever, executing justice
> for the exploited and giving food to the hun-
> gry. The LORD frees prisoners. The LORD opens
> the eyes of the blind. The LORD raises up those
> who are **oppressed**. The LORD loves the righ-
> teous. (Ps. 146:6b–8)

> The one who **oppresses** the poor person
> insults his Maker, but one who is kind to the
> needy honors him. (Prov. 14:31)

> "The Spirit of the Lord is on me, because he
> has anointed me to preach good news to the
> poor. He has sent me to proclaim release to the
> captives and recovery of sight to the blind, to
> set free the **oppressed**." (Luke 4:18)

The oppression described in Scripture ranges from human
slavery to financial injustice to persecution, demonstrating
that God is against all coercion, brutality, injustice, exploita-
tion, and abuse. Oppression encompasses sexual, physical,
emotional, verbal, and spiritual abuse, and it could be a one-
time experience or repeated, chronic oppression. You might

feel like it's somehow your fault, but it's not. You are *not* responsible for *someone else's* choices.

I encounter many women who are hesitant to label their experience as abuse because it does not match what others have experienced or because it does not align with their mental definition of abuse. Or they might consider their experience(s) "too low-grade" to be abuse, thinking that abuse means being hit, raped, or something violent.

In such situations, I've pulled out a list of abusive behaviors or a list of thoughts and feelings commonly experienced by abuse victims, giving the person space to locate themselves within those lists.[2] In these conversations, I will call abuse what it is, but it can take time for some people to acknowledge that what they've experienced is actually abuse. However, it's affirming to survivors for people to acknowledge that what's been done to them is evil and hated by God.

God and Your Abuse

I'm often hesitant to respond to a survivor's faith questions. It takes a lot of listening and asking God for discernment to know when it's the time to simply be a safe hearer of their questions and when it's time to answer them. I wrestle with this in every such conversation.

One day, a young woman and I were driving, and the conversation suddenly went deep as she questioned, "Where was God when my abuser abused me—and not only me but several other children as well?"

Accompanying this question were others about why God allows some people to experience more suffering than others and why He allows sin to perpetuate in a family *for generations.*

While this young woman genuinely wanted answers to her questions, I also recognized that this particular conversation was *not* the time to launch into a theological lecture on suffering. Did she need me to explain sin, suffering, and God's will, or did she need something else in this moment? As I listened to her questions, I simultaneously prayed for wisdom with my words, desiring *not* to inadvertently be like Job's friends in my response.

For this conversation, I chose not to answer her questions directly but to relay how God can understand abuse because, as Christ the Son, He experienced it firsthand. Being tortured and crucified, Jesus endured physical assault at the hands of others. He experienced ridicule, verbal threats, and betrayal by someone close to Him. While Jesus was not sexually abused, He was sexually humiliated when He hung naked on the cross with Roman soldiers gambling for His garments. He too suffered and survived severe trauma, bearing its scars in His body.

In Isaiah 52:13–53:12, the prophet foretold of Jesus, the Suffering Servant, and described how He would be treated:

- Hurt so badly he was disfigured and unrecognizable (52:14)
- Despised (53:3)
- Rejected (53:3)
- Experientially familiar with suffering and grief (53:3)
- Not valued by people, considered insignificant (53:3)
- Unaided in His suffering—people responded to it with astonishment, judgment, or apathy (52:14; 53:3, 4, 8)
- Misunderstood, with people thinking His suffering was somehow deserved (53:4)
- Pierced (53:5)
- Crushed severely (53:5, 10)
- Punished for something He did not do (53:5)

- Wounded (53:5)
- Oppressed (53:7)
- Afflicted (53:7)
- Oppressively judged (53:8)
- Struck (53:8)
- Killed (53:8)
- Anguished (53:11)
- Wrongly counted as a sinner (53:12)

Do you identify with anything on this list? This text demonstrates that Jesus knows what it's like to be abused. Jesus experienced such sorrow and grief because He bore ours: "Surely he has borne our griefs and carried our sorrows."[3] He can empathize with you not just because He is all-knowing and has experienced abuse; He has carried *your* grief and *your* sorrow.

Our grief and sorrow—as well as our sin—was transferred to Him on the cross.[4] He felt all of it when He bore the weight of every sin that ever has been and ever will be committed. He personally knows the horror of every atrocity perpetrated by man because it was placed on Him at the cross. In order to redeem the world, the Suffering Servant shared in the suffering of this world. The One who came to set the oppressed free experienced oppression Himself.

At the center of the gospel is the abuse of our Savior. This implies that your abuse matters to God. Your pain matters to God. Your questions matter to Him. Your emotions matter to Him. Your body and what has been done to it matters to Him. *You* matter to Him.

With this foundation in place, the next appendix explores how trauma affects you.

A Word on Trauma

WHETHER ABUSE OCCURRED AS AN ISOLATED INCIDENT OR OVER time, trauma leaves its mark in every facet of your life. Even if you consider your circumstances "minor" compared to others, this isn't about comparison; it's about accounting for what has been done *to you*. Trauma wounds you physically, emotionally, relationally, and spiritually, and as we examine these four categories of trauma's effects, I'll also address the family members, friends, and mentors who are journeying alongside an abuse survivor.

Physical Effects

Physical Symptoms

Poor concentration, insomnia, headaches, fatigue, chronic pain, weight loss, stomach pain, diarrhea, nausea—these are all ways trauma affects the body. A survivor may not be talking about their trauma, but their body often speaks for them. It's not unusual for anniversaries, stress, or certain places or smells to trigger these physical symptoms. Working through trauma can also exacerbate physical symptoms, and while symptoms may subside, they can suddenly reemerge if triggered. While a survivor can experience God's restoration and peace, they can't erase or forget what has happened, and their body feels the effects of their memories and emotions.

For the Alongsider: You will feel helpless when a survivor tells you about their physical anguish, and your best recommendations of products (Essential Oils, Tylenol, Pepto-Bismol, etc.) won't help because their physical symptoms are rooted in their trauma. It's how their body is dealing with the hurt they've experienced, and while you can't fix their physical symptoms, you can listen to them, pray, encourage, and meet physical needs. If there's food they *can* eat, bring it to them, or offer to go to the store for them if it's a particularly hard week. Find ways to serve them and let them know they're not alone.

Hypervigilance

Many survivors are constantly on alert, expecting danger. For the survivor, hypervigilance is like a sensitive car alarm that continually goes off, even when no one is near the car, and a hypervigilant person's adrenal glands constantly produce adrenaline and noradrenalin, which prime the body for an emergency even when there is none. Hypervigilance leaves a person feeling physically and emotionally drained, and with this, survivors may avoid crowded places or big groups because they don't feel safe and can't rest while there.

For the Alongsider: While you can't change these responses in a person's brain, you can be sensitive to them. For example, survivors may not feel comfortable attending large gatherings, so don't pressure them to do so. It's their choice. Hypervigilance makes it easy to isolate, so plan opportunities where they can be with people in a setting that feels more controlled and safe to them. Recognize that hypervigilance may also affect their willingness to go to church. I've helped several young women strategically plan where they'll park, when they'll arrive and leave, what door they'll enter, where they'll sit, and who they'll sit with in order to accommodate their needs and help them feel safe.

Intrusions and Triggers

Many survivors will relive their trauma through intrusions such as flashbacks and night terrors. When a person is triggered, remembering certain memories or details of the abuse makes it feel as though the danger is happening all over again. Because of how trauma memories are stored in the brain, a survivor re-experiences in the first person what they remember, which can be disorienting and painful. While some triggers (smells, sounds, sights, words, or feelings) can be identified, others are like landmines. You don't know it's a trigger until you step on it.

I encourage survivors to create a list of twenty-five healthy, self-soothing activities they can do if they're triggered or wake up from a night terror. By preidentifying a list of things, if one doesn't work, they can try the next thing on the list. (This is also helpful for when struggling with temptation!)

For the Alongsider: Several of the survivors I know have "self-care baskets" that include items they can use to self-soothe in productive ways. Items include stress balls, sensory putty, weighted blankets, night lights, journal, note cards with reassuring Scriptures or quotes, encouraging notes they've received, heating pad, puzzles, a favorite candy, bubble wrap, exercise ball, candles or oils, a soothing CD, a favorite calming movie or book, a craft to make, coloring books, etc. Consider contributing items to their basket or writing notes filled with truth that they can keep and re-read.

If you're present when a flashback or night terror occurs, speak calmly, refrain from touching them until they come to, and gently remind them of where they are. You can also ask them what they smell, hear, smell, or see to ground them in reality. Offer to sit with them and do a self-soothing activity together such as watching a movie, playing a board game, or doing a craft. You can't prevent their intrusions, but you can minister to them with your calming presence.

Emotional Effects

Because trauma overwhelms, many survivors consciously or subconsciously attempt to avoid all things emotional. They numb themselves, stifle their feelings, or engage in escaping behaviors (over-working, binging on TV, gaming, self harm, substance abuse, porn, etc.) in order to avoid their memories and emotions. These behaviors mute the emotions for a little while but lack the ability to suppress them forever.

Another form of avoidance is dissociation, which involves detaching from the trauma while it occurs or when triggered. While dissociating during the abuse enables a person to endure physically by separating mentally through imagination or trance-like states,[1] survivors will later find themselves disassociating in every day life, for they'll space out during conversations or events, unaware of what is occurring around them. What enabled them to endure the abuse while it happened inhibits them from being present for their own lives long after the abuse has ended.

It's understandable that someone would try to avoid remembering the horror they've endured, and it's reasonable that a person would develop strategies to help them cope with their trauma memories. But we can't deal with what lives in the shadows. While a survivor may not want to revisit their trauma, doing so will be necessary for them to heal, and such work will take time, necessitate support from their community, and require professional help.

As a survivor courageously begins confronting trauma, she will feel overwhelmed. Trauma therapist Diane Langberg notes, "Feelings express what the trauma did to the victim just like the blood shows what a cut did to the skin. . . . Feelings are the expression of the wounds of the heart."[2]

Fear, grief, anger, guilt—these emotions, among others, accompany trauma. A survivor may feel angry that someone would violate her or allow her to continue being violated. She may feel angry at herself for not speaking up, for not stopping the abuse, for how her body responded to touch, for caring for her abuser despite what they've done, etc. She may feel fear about the future, of losing control, of being in crowds, of small spaces, or of being alone. She may feel grief over what she's lost or what she never got to experience, and she may feel guilt as though she's somehow responsible for her abuse.

Feelings of shame also accompany abuse. Shame involves how we see ourselves in light of what we've done or what's been done to us. Because of abuse, shame might leave a survivor seeing herself as other, unworthy, trashed, unclean, or worthless.

For survivors of abuse, you are *not* at fault for what's been done to you, and while you may feel shame, *the shame belongs to your oppressor, NOT you.* Your abuser's actions reflect on him/her, *not* on you. Their actions show what is in their hearts, not yours. You did *not* deserve what happened to you, and you are not at fault for what *someone else* chooses to do, no matter what you were wearing, where you were, or whom you were with. Dealing with shame begins by accounting for what you have done and delineating it from what others have done to you. With abuse, shame would have you take the blame for everything, but your abuser's sin is *not* your sin.

For the Alongsider: It's not uncommon for survivors to cope with their trauma in unproductive ways. While survivors do need to learn healthy ways to respond, we need to triage as we walk alongside them. What is their greatest need at this particular time? Are we listening and understanding *their* particular experience of suffering? Are they resourced to deal with the effects of their trauma? If not, connect them to people and resources. They need safety and stabilization in order to process their trauma, so this is first priority. While learning *healthy* ways to cope is important, this takes time to learn and to implement, and as they take steps, they'll need your grace and encouragement, not your condemnation and legalism. Focus on their safety and stabilization before you zero in on any of their sinful coping mechanisms.

Be aware that a survivor might avoid the very people who are trying to help her deal with her trauma. I've seen ladies cancel appointments with their counselors or mentors because they wanted to put off conversations or not be asked how they're really doing. Continue to encourage, affirm, and pursue them, not letting them slip through the cracks. If you haven't heard from them in awhile, check in. If they tell you they missed an appointment with a psychiatrist, counselor, or doctor, ask why and gently encourage them to make another appointment.

If a woman chooses to tell you about her abuse, that means she sees you as a safe person, so be a conscientious steward of that trust. Thank her for trusting you and affirm the courage it took for her to voice what happened.

What do you say when someone courageously tells you of their assault? A few helpful responses include:

- I'm so sorry this happened to you.
- I believe you.
- Thank you for telling me.
- What happened is not your fault.

- You're not the only one who has responded this way. You're not crazy.
- You don't have to deal with this alone.
- There's hope. Things can get better. You can get better.

While you may hear details of a survivor's story that concern you such as their language, their clothing, their location, their use of substances, or their association with questionable characters, the time for addressing such things is *not* at the moment of their disclosure, for in addressing these things at disclosure, you inadvertently blame them for being victimized. Even if they did sin or were unwise in some way, the time to address such things will come later. We begin by compassionately caring for their wounds, giving them time to heal. With our words and actions at such a vulnerable time, we want to accurately reflect God's care for them.

If you're not trained in trauma-informed care, don't press a survivor for details about their abuse, for you don't need to know them. Counselors, doctors, lawyers, police investigators, social workers, and Child Protective Services—they're the ones who need to know the details. Let survivors tell you what they want to tell you, if and when they want to tell you.

Also, know that it's common for survivors to have memory gaps about their trauma, and as a result, they can appear mentally unstable, contradictory, or confused about what happened. They may even laugh or make jokes about it. As a result, your first instinct will likely be to question their story. But err on the side of believing the survivor, and if possible, keep your voice even, your body language open, and your movements slow in the conversation in order to help her feel safe.

Common feelings of victims include fear about what will happen to them, concern over whether or not they'll be believed, self-doubt about whether they're overreacting to what they've experienced, shame about what has been done

to them, and lies about the abuse being their fault or something they somehow deserve. Be careful not to reinforce these
lies and negative emotions. Affirm their value. Affirm that what
has happened to them is evil, wrong, and grieves the heart of
God. Affirm that they are not responsible for someone violating
them. For a variety of reasons, survivors may downplay what
happened to them, not even calling it abuse, but we should
name abuse what it is—sin (and in many cases, a crime).

Relational Effects

Relationships are already complicated because of our own
sinfulness. Furthermore, we all have baggage because of past
experiences and relationships, and trauma adds one more bag
to the pile. A survivor recently told me that her shorthand for
this is #traumanotdrama. While she may feel like she's being
dramatic about something, she's not, because what she's experiencing are the effects of trauma.

Because abuse happens with people, it affects how we view
and relate to people, and two unhealthy responses I commonly
see include unhealthily pursuing relationships and fearfully
avoiding relationships. The **unhealthy pursuit of relationships** can occur in friendships, romantic relationships, hook-
ups, or within the family of origin. Perhaps a survivor assumes
she can't refuse when asked or told to do something. Perhaps
she's so needy for affirmation or a sense of significance that
she grasps for it wherever she can. Perhaps she longs to be
touched and wanted. Perhaps she desires to be safe and pro-
tected and ignores warning signs (or perhaps alarms don't
even go off) because of how abuse has shaped her.

With this, beware of codependency. This occurs when
one person, the codependent, allows the needs of the other
to rule them, leading them to sacrifice their own well-being
in order to "satisfy" the other person. Meanwhile, the other

party uses the relationship to define their sense of security and self-esteem. Boundaries do not exist or are not respected, and each person attempts to use or control the other in various ways. Manipulation and neediness abound in such relationships as both people attempt to fit a square person-sized peg into a round God-sized hole.

Because abusers do not respect boundaries, survivors, especially those who experienced abuse as children, often do not learn them. A person may also be worn down over time by an abuser who repeatedly disregards their no and bulldozes over them. Because they felt out of control when abused, survivors may try to control their relationships to ensure their needs are met, that they're not hurt again, and that their voice is heard. They may not consider how their controlling behavior affects others, and they may not even recognize what they're doing. Either way, broken relationships usually lie in their wake.

When it comes to **fearfully avoiding relationships**, it's understandable that, for example, abuse by a man would lead a survivor to be wary of men. As a result, relationships with women might feel safer and more comfortable, with such feelings becoming twisted and leading to homosexual behavior. While abuse can contribute to someone's same-sex attraction, abuse does *not* always result in homosexuality, and not every same-sex attracted person has abuse in their story.

While some survivors have no boundaries in their relationships, others maintain strict ones. Emotional walls are up, and most of their friends as well as the people they date remain unsuccessful at scaling them. Trust in relationships requires risk, and that risk of being hurt again leads some survivors to relationally keep people at a distance as a self-protection mechanism.

I see this play out with many of the college and young single women I walk alongside. They want to date and marry, but they fear being abused again. They question whether or not someone would ever want to marry them after learning about their abuse and what it's like to live with a survivor. I've also seen many survivors get married and quickly realize ways in which their past abuse affects their marriage, even though their husband is nothing like their abuser.

If this is you, you *can* experience healthy relationships, even if you've never known one in the past. You *can* learn how to distinguish between safe people and unsafe people. You *can* learn how to engage in godly relational patterns and how to maintain healthy boundaries. You *can* learn to trust, as scary as it may seem, and you *can* learn how to identify trustworthy people.

Abuse gives us dysfunctional blueprints for how to relate to one another, but the Bible provides commands and examples of God's blueprints for healthy relationships. Texts such as 1 Corinthians 13; Philippians 2; Ephesians 5:22–6:9; Colossians 3:18–4:1; and the "one another" commands in the New Testament explain how we're to relate to each other. We can practice these traits in our lives, and knowing them can also help us identify safe people around us.

For the Alongsider: When I'm meeting with young women, experience has taught me to look for test balloons in conversations. It's a common self-protection mechanism to gauge reactions and trustworthiness with a "lighter" issue before sharing something more personal, and our responses to people either build trust or break it.

Mental health issues alone do not mean that someone has trauma in their story, but because it *could* be part of their story, it's something I listen for as I get to know a person. The same goes with addictions, eating disorders, and sexual sin— those sin struggles do not necessarily mean that someone has trauma in their story, but it *could* be.

If a couple alludes to intimacy issues, have it on your radar that abuse might be a contributing factor. If someone disso-ciated when being sexually abused, it's not surprising that they'd dissociate when having sex with their spouse. A sur-vivor's *body* might respond to their spouse the same way it responded to an abuser, even though their *mind* recognizes that their spouse is not their abuser. So bear this in mind as a possibility, and know that addressing trauma will be necessary for the couple's sexual relationship to improve.

If you suspect abuse, lean in and ask. The following ques-tions can be helpful follow-ups in conversation:

- Have you ever been an unwilling partici-pant in a sexual act?
- Have you ever been touched in any way that made you uncomfortable?
- Have you ever been threatened or physi-cally hurt?
- Do you ever feel fearful around your spouse (or boyfriend, fiancé, parent, sib-ling, etc.)?
- Do you feel like you're constantly walking on eggshells in an effort not to upset them?
- If married, do you not have the freedom to be yourself? To make decisions? To give your input? To disagree?

If they answer "yes" to any of these questions, inquire if they've ever worked through what they've experienced. If not, ask if this is something they'd like to do, letting them know you're available as a friend to support them in the process.

Sometimes people will allude to trauma being part of their story. If they do, follow up privately. Ask if it's something they would like to talk about, and offer to listen if they ever do want to talk. If they've not processed their hurt, offer to connect them to resources. However, don't push them to do anything. Invite them, but don't push them. Express your care for them, and follow up to check in on how they're doing.

If the person is *currently* in an abusive situation, their safety is the number one priority, but know that you can inadvertently put a victim in more danger if you handle this incorrectly. With minors, report any abuse to Child Protective Services or to the police department. Even if you *suspect* abuse, report it. Reasonable suspicion serves as the threshold for reporting abuse in good faith.[3] It's *not* your job to investigate or confirm the abuse before reporting. By reporting, you're requesting that a situation be investigated by those who are trained to interview minors, identify predatory behavior, and act on the results of an investigation.

With an adult, this is a different story. Obtaining restraining orders and pressing charges remain the adult's choice and is not something to be done lightly since these actions can incite an abuser and put a victim in great danger. Reporting also requires a survivor to tell about their abuse, which can be incredibly difficult, and they are not guaranteed that their interviewer will believe them or respond well to them.

If an adult confides in you about an ongoing abusive situation, assess whether she has a safe place to sleep. Is it safe for her to go about her day? If she lives with her abuser, does she need help creating a safety plan to leave her situation? Does she need help securing her safety, and if so, who are the appropriate people to help her with this? If she does need help or if you have questions about what to do, local and national hotlines are available, including the National Domestic Violence Hotline (1-800-799-SAFE) and the National Sexual Assault Hotline (1-800-656-HOPE). Utilize these services to formulate a plan that considers all the variables of her particular situation. Furthermore, do not confront the abuser, especially if they still have the opportunity to hurt the person, for the most dangerous time for a victim is when they are considering leaving and right after they leave.[4]

With all of this, do *not* make decisions for the survivor. Her abuser dominated her and did not respect her voice; don't do the same. Give her options, and respect her ability to choose, even if you do not agree with her choice. Also, know it can take time for someone to acknowledge their abuse and be at a point where they're willing to leave, especially with the manipulation and gaslighting that often occurs in abusive relationships.

Spiritual Effects

How can a loving, good God let me be abused? How can God be just when nobody believes my disclosure or when my abuser lives freely? Why did God let me be born if He knew this would happen to me? Where is His purpose in this? How can He be trusted when He's let *this* happen to me?

When a person's circumstances do not jive with what the Bible teaches about God's love, goodness, and justice, do not be surprised if they question God. But know that He's big enough to handle our questions and is not mad at us for asking them. He doesn't respond to questions the way an abuser would.

During a class on Psalms in seminary, my Hebrew professor assigned Psalm 22 to me for my semester-long project. A psalm of lament, Psalm 22 questions why God has not answered the psalmist's prayers and why He seems to have forsaken him. Lament psalms guide us in how to converse with God about the things we can't make sense of in this world. In laments, the worshiper asks God, "Why?" "How long?" "When?" "Where?" and boldly commands Him to do something about the situation.

In Psalm 22, the circumstances King David describes involve physical danger, intimidation, mockery, abandonment,

and abuse. In all of this, David vacillates between questioning God (vv. 1–2) and reminding himself of God's character
(v. 3). He recounts God's faithfulness to His people in the past
(vv. 4–5) then pendulum-swings to lamenting his situation
(vv. 6–8) before swinging back to describe God's faithfulness
in his own life (vv. 9–10). Then, he recounts more details of
his oppression and its effects on him (vv. 10–18). The psalmist confesses what he knows to be true about God, even while
describing the painful and unjust circumstances God has
allowed to happen to him.

With the lament psalms, the psalmist's questions and cries
to God stem from faith *in* God. Throughout Psalm 22, David petitions the Lord even as he questions Him, which demonstrates
an undercurrent of trust in the psalmist's life. This instructs us
in how to process our own questions and suffering.

If you're a survivor of abuse, you might find it challenging
to read the Bible or talk to God, but if you're willing to start,
begin with Psalms and find your questions in the laments. Use
the lament psalms as a guide for processing your own questions and pain with God. To do this, take one of these psalms,
and follow its outline as a guide for writing your own lament
to God. Replace the psalmist's question with your question,
his description of circumstances with yours, and his petitions
with yours. When the psalmist describes God's character or
points to times of God's faithfulness, do the same.

You might also be in a season where you find it to difficult to pray or engage in spiritual disciplines. When the group
of survivors sat around my table to offer feedback on caring
well, one young woman acknowledged that she often experiences dry seasons and feels guilty for not being "a very good
Christian." This connects to her faith questions and her struggle to believe truth about God. On one hand, she gets mad
at God for the abuse He's allowed her to experience, and on
the other hand, she wants Him to comfort and restore her.

Confusion and questions about God can be even harder to sort through if an abuser claims to be a Christian, talks about God, or quotes Scripture.

Often, Christian survivors feel external or internal pressure to forgive their abuser. At the same time, they may not want to forgive them. Although anger toward an abuser is understandable, carrying anger, bitterness, and resentment comes at an emotional cost, wearing a person down, and a survivor will continue to be tied to their abuser until they relinquish their anger—and the abuser—to God.

With this, let's clarify what biblical forgiveness entails.

Trauma and Forgiveness

Forgiveness is a process.

Forgiveness requires acknowledging the pain we've experienced rather than stuffing or minimizing it. The sin committed against us must be recognized for the evil it is, not glossed over. Forgiveness does not diminish the evil that's been done, for the wickedness must be acknowledged in order to be forgiven.

If we do not want to forgive, this is an area where we need the Holy Spirit to change our heart, and meditating on God's forgiveness of us motivates us to extend forgiveness to others. But this can be hard because of the hurt experienced, especially if the offender doesn't acknowledge or care that their sin affected you. With this, forgiveness is a process because sanctification is a process.

Forgiveness does not mean forgetting.

Forgiveness does not imply "getting over" what happened. Instead, it's choosing how you'll think about the person who has hurt you. When your abuser comes to mind, will you mentally replay how they've hurt you? Will you allow this loop to stir up your anger toward them, or will you replace it, focusing instead on their need for God and maybe even praying for them?

Forgiveness is something we continue to choose each time they come to mind. With Christians, our all-knowing God does not forget our sin; instead, He chooses to remember Christ, the substitute for our sins. Therefore, He sees us as clean and righteous, not as sinners. The difference here is how God thinks of us because of Christ.

Forgiveness and reconciliation are two different things.

Forgiving your abuser does *not* necessarily mean you must reconcile and reenter a relationship with them, for reconciliation may not be possible, wise, or safe for a variety of reasons. Do not equate forgiveness with a lack of common sense about an unsafe person.

With God, only those who believe and *repent* experience reconciliation with Him. In describing heaven, Jennifer Greenberg notes, "Heaven is described as a city with strong walls—borders impassable to God's enemies. God does not allow the unrepentant in his presence, and abusers need not be permitted in ours."[5]

Forgiveness does not negate justice.

We can forgive someone and still pursue justice against them. Sin has consequences, and forgiveness does not cancel out those consequences. For example, consider King David's sin with Bathsheba (which many interpret as a sexually abusive act). David later repented and sought God's forgiveness, and although God forgave him, the prophet Nathan informed David that there would also be consequences for his actions (2 Sam. 11–12).

We should not treat forgiveness as though it is more important than justice. Both are equally important to God. In fact, God's justice had to be accounted for in order for our forgiveness to be possible. At the very cross that enables our forgiveness, God administered justice, for when Christ absorbed God's wrath against sin on the cross, He paid our sin debt with His life.

Raised in an emotionally and verbally abusive home, the young woman across the table from me bemoaned the lack of consequences her mother experiences. No one outside the home knows the truth about what she's like, and this young woman expressed frustration that outsiders consider her mother to be a "good Christian woman" when she's actually a manipulative, controlling bully. Such injustice hinders her from forgiving her mom.

How does the Bible speak to the lack of justice we often see on earth? When describing Jesus' death, 1 Peter 2:23 states, "when he was insulted, he did not insult in return; when he suffered, he did not threaten but entrusted himself to the one who judges justly." The people who flogged Jesus, thrust the crown of thorns on His head, and pushed for Him to be crucified—what justice did they face for these actions while on earth? The Roman soldiers did not get sent to prison for abusing an innocent man. The Jewish religious leaders did not face public censure for their actions, and after calling for Jesus' crucifixion, the jeering crowd simply went home after His death. Life went on as usual for all of these people, even though they allowed Jesus to suffer unjustly and participated in His abuse. Peter points back to this event and expresses that Jesus "entrusted himself to the one who judges justly." Jesus trusted God to exact justice against His oppressors.

Because God is a righteous and just Judge, He will not let sin go unpunished. All sin will be accounted for—either by Christ's death on the cross or by the individual as they

experience eternal torment. We can have hope, even if abusers do not face justice on earth, for they will give an account
of their sin to God (Rom. 14:10–12; 2 Cor. 5:10). The assurance
that God will punish the sin of your abuser frees you to forgive
(Rom. 12:19–21). God's wrath against sin offers great hope to
those victimized by sin, for He will bring justice in His perfect
timing and way.

For the Alongsider: As you converse with a survivor, you
might feel uncomfortable with the emotions they express or
the questions they ask, but in the best interest of the survivor,
do not rush in to correct. Instead, give them space to express
what they think and feel. We can't deal with things that we
don't bring to light, so if they trust you enough to open up to
you, listen. Let them share and emote without you trying to
fix them, offer spiritual platitudes, or tell them "at least" their
circumstances aren't as bad as someone else's.

In her book *Suffering and the Heart of God*, Diane Langberg
relays three components necessary for trauma recovery: talking, tears, and time.[6] It often takes time for someone to voice
what's happened. Whether they tell their story to you or someone else, they will need to express the facts of what happened
as well as their feelings in order to heal.

If you're in their life, you'll watch them experience a roller
coaster of emotions as they deal with their trauma. You'll see
them ebb and flow emotionally, overwhelmed with emotion
(the flow) and subsequently numbing out (the ebb). When I
explain this to women, I compare it to a gallon challenge. If
you've never observed a gallon challenge, each participant
has one gallon of milk, which they must drink *in one hour*.
Within that hour, the participant inevitably throws up because
their body cannot absorb that much calcium in such a short
time frame.

Similarly, it takes time to process trauma. It can be done,
but it happens best when the survivor paces herself and

doesn't feel constrained to do things within a particular time frame. How do we deal with trauma? Like how one best completes the gallon challenge, one sip at a time—and without the time constraint! Recovery takes patience and entails repetition, telling the story and feeling the emotions again and again. Why? Because of the magnitude of what's been done. It takes time for words to come, for feelings to be expressed and understood, for trust to occur, and for wounds to heal. Recovery can't be rushed, no matter how much it hurts to work through the trauma.

As a survivor shares, you'll likely hear incorrect theology or misconceptions they have about a number of subjects. You might hear them express feelings that are sinful or that strike a minor chord, and you'll also hear dissonance as they express both faith and unbelief in the same conversation. How do you walk alongside them? What do you respond to first?

Triage here. Discern between symptoms and roots, and focus on the roots. As you do root work, many of the symptoms will eventually resolve themselves. It's also essential to consider the stability of the person. I recently met with one survivor who's in a rough patch of not sleeping because of night terrors and anxiety, and because of her distressed state and lack of sleep, I recommended pulling back from trauma work in order to regain some stability with sleep. Dealing with trauma is playing the long game, and the survivor needs to feel safe and stable in order to continue doing the work.

Gauge the emotional state of the survivor as you consider whether to bring up an issue that you see. Assess whether now is the time to bring it up, and since you do not know the hearts or minds of people, pray for the Spirit to give you guidance in what to say and when to say it. Beware of treating the survivor as a project. Instead, care for them as a *person*.

As I meet with a girl and assess where she is, I note a few areas to address, and *over the course* of a mentoring relationship with her, that assessment helps me be strategic and intentional in my meetings with her. However, I don't let that dictate every conversation I have with her. With girls I disciple, I'll mix in conversations or activities that are light-hearted with conversations about their spiritual growth. I care about the *whole* person and want them to feel that, which would not be the case if I'm constantly correcting and bringing up things they need to work on. I don't need to be their Holy Spirit. He already exists, and I'm not Him. He's called me to be faithful in the relationship, to pray for the person, and to give space for the Holy Spirit to do His work in His time.

If a survivor shares with you, you have insight that few, if any other, people have about how to pray for them. Be diligent in lifting up the specific aspects of their story that they've relayed to you. This might be the very reason God has called you to be a witness to their story and how He wants you to serve them the most. So do not overlook the ministry of prayer as you walk alongside survivors.

Abuse Is Not the End of Your Story

Abuse may be part of your story, but it's not the end of your story if you're a Christ-follower. In Revelation 21, the apostle John relays a God-given vision of the new heavens and the new earth. In a season where I was feeling the weight of several abuse disclosures, I reflected on this text in light of oppression.

Revelation 21 describes a coming day when perfect justice will be handed out—the day when "the cowards, faithless, detestable, murderers, sexually immoral, sorcerers, idolaters, and all liars"[7] will face ultimate judgment for their sins in the lake of fire.

On that day, there will be complete safety and perfect peace because the new Jerusalem will be a place where

"Nothing unclean will ever enter it, nor anyone who does what is detestable or false, but only those written in the Lamb's book of life."[8]

On that day, there will be no darkness and no sin. Everything will exist in the light, and God will be the source of that light: ". . . because the glory of God illuminates it, and its lamp is the Lamb."[9]

On that day . . .

- There will be no more night terrors or tears.
- No more counseling sessions or medications to help with sleep, anxiety, or depression.
- No more flashbacks, triggers, or panic attacks.
- Nor more need for security systems, restraining orders, or looking over your shoulder.
- No more fear of seeing your abuser or knowing they're out there with the ability to hurt others.
- No more shame or guilt or feeling vulnerable.

On that day, ". . . God himself will be with them and will be their God. He will wipe away every tear from their eyes. Death will be no more; grief, crying, and pain will be no more, because the previous things have passed away. Then the one seated on the throne said, 'Look, I am making everything new.'"[10]

Acknowledgments

TO MY PARENTS AND BROTHER, THANK YOU FOR LISTENING AS I've processed countless ministry situations, for praying with me over the phone, for supporting me, and for encouraging me to persevere in times that ministry has been hard. Much of what I've learned about ministry and discipleship has been shaped by what I learned and saw happening at home. I love y'all and am so incredibly grateful for our family of 'Nuts!

Thank you to my friends, encouragers, and prayer warriors. The notes written, the texts and Marco Polos sent, the tea and coffee provided, the dinners eaten together as writing breaks, and the prayers prayed kept me going during the writing and editing of this book.

Thank you to Dr. Tate Cockrell, who (along with my mom) was one of the first people to suggest I write this book and who prodded me to go back to school for biblical counseling.

Thank you to The church at Brook Hills for financially supporting my counseling studies at SEBTS and for investing in me. God has used my time in Birmingham and at Brook Hills to shape me as a disciple-maker and Christ-follower, and I am so incredibly thankful for my Brook Hills faith family.

For the women who are referenced in this book, thank you for trusting me with your stories, and thank you for letting me include them so that other women will know they're not the only ones who struggle.

Thank you to the ladies who served as readers of various chapters. Your expertise as counselors, recovery group leaders/sponsors, and writers sharpened the content in this book.

Thank you to Kelly King for allowing me to continue serving as a Lifeway Women's Trainer, for graciously letting me send you some sample chapters, and for connecting me to the publishing team at B&H. Thank you to Mary Wiley for sending me the sample book proposal and for passing along the proposal for this book. Thank you to the fabulous marketing team at B&H Publishing, and thank you to my editor, Ashley Gorman, who guided me through this whole process and who provided invaluable feedback, encouragement, and help in shaping this manuscript.

Notes

Chapter 2: Why We're Broken: Part I

1. Bryan Chapell, *Christ-Centered Preaching*, 2nd ed. (Grand Rapids: Baker Academic, 2005), 277.
2. Psalm 14:3
3. English Standard Version
4. Matthew 6:13 ESV
5. Matthew 26:41 ESV
6. Romans 7:15, 18b–19 (CSB), 21–23 (NIV)
7. Hebrews 4:15
8. Matthew 6:12, 13 ESV
9. 1 Corinthians 10:13
10. 2 Corinthians 12:9a
11. James 1:14 ESV
12. Paul David Tripp, *Instruments in the Redeemer's Hands* (Phillipsburg, NJ: P&R Publishing Company, 2002), 68.
13. Class notes from "Biblical Counseling" by Dr. Steven P. Wade at Southeastern Baptist Theological Seminary, Spring 2016.
14. To clarify here, telling a lie or disobeying authority does not flood a brain with dopamine the way that engaging in addictive behavior does. But when you sin (whether or not it's sexual sin), you are, on some level, associating that sin with pleasure or pleasurable results, which encourages you to repeat the behavior.
15. Edward Welch, *Blame It on the Brain* (Phillipsburg, NJ: Presbyterian and Reformed Publishing Company, 1998), 167.
16. James 4:6 ESV
17. English Standard Version

Chapter 3: Why We're Broken: Part 2

1. Dr. Henry Cloud and Dr. John Townsend, *Boundaries* (Grand Rapids: Zondervan, 1992), 64.
2. H. Norman Wright, *Making Peace with Your Past* (Grand Rapids: Fleming H. Revell, 1985), 39.
3. Psalm 34:18 ESV

4. Psalm 147:3

5. Ephesians 6:12

6. See 1 Timothy 4:1; 2 Corinthians 2:11; 4:4; James 2:19; Matthew 8:31; Luke 8:30; Revelation 20:10; Ephesians 6:10–12.

7. English Standard Version

8. Matthew 6:13 ESV

Chapter 4: The God Who Designed Us

1. Genesis 2:18–20

2. Genesis 2:18

3. Genesis 2:18

4. Jen Wilkin, "Session Four: Created in the Image of God," *God of Creation: A Study of Genesis 1–11* (Nashville: LifeWay, 2018).

5. Andrew Walker, *God and the Transgender Debate* (Charlotte, NC: The Good Book Company, 2017), 51–52.

6. Psalm 16:11

7. George Müller quoted in John Piper, *Desiring God* (Sisters: Multnomah Publishers, Inc., 2003), 142.

8. 1 Corinthians 6:18–20

9. Eugene Monroe Bartlett, "Victory in Jesus" (1939).

10. 1 Corinthians 6:19

Chapter 5: Why Sexual Sin Is Sin: Sex Is Heterosexual

1. David Platt, "The Cross and Christian Sexuality—Part 1," June 23, 2013, https://radical.net/sermon/the-cross-and-christian-sexuality-part-1/. David Platt, "The Cross and Christian Sexuality—Part 2," June 30, 2013, https://radical.net/sermon/the-cross-and-christian-sexuality-part-2/.

2. I later learned that my pastor's sermons on 1 Corinthians 6 were heavily influenced by Daniel R. Heimbach's book *True Sexual Morality*, so I am also grateful for his teaching on God's design for sex.

3. English Standard Version

4. Rosaria Champagne Butterfield, *The Secret Thoughts of an Unlikely Convert* (Pittsburgh: Crown & Covenant Publications, 2012), 31.

5. John Piper, *Sex and the Supremacy of Christ*, ed. John Piper and Justin Taylor (Wheaton: Crossway, 2005), 26.

6. Sam Allberry, *7 Myths about Singleness* (Wheaton: Crossway, 2019), 120.

7. Kevin DeYoung, *What Does the Bible Really Teach about Homosexuality?* (Wheaton: Crossway, 2015), 32.

8. Daniel Heimbach, *True Sexual Morality* (Wheaton: Crossway, 2004), 170.

9. For more on Leviticus 20, I found chapter 3 of Kevin DeYoung's book *What Does the Bible Really Teach about Homosexuality?* to be helpful.

10. Romans 1:24

11. Jackie Hill Perry, *Gay Girl, Good God* (Nashville: B&H Publishing Group, 2018), 20.

12. Romans 1:32

Chapter 6: Why Sexual Sin Is Sin: Sex Is Relational

1. David Platt, "Christ, Culture, and a Call to Action—Session 3," July 30, 2018, https://vimeo.com/282292817#t=1h6m45s or https://radical.net/?session=christ-culture-and-a-call-to-action-session-3.

2. C. S. Lewis, Letter to Keith Masson on June 3, 1956, *Yours, Jack: The Inspirational Letters of C. S. Lewis ed.* Paul F. Ford (London: Harper, 2008), 292–93.

3. Matthew 5:27–28

4. Walter Bauer, *A Greek-English Lexicon of the New Testament and Other Early Christian Literature*, rev. and ed. Frederick W. Danker, 3rd ed. (Chicago: University of Chicago Press: 2000), 371–72.

5. J. I. Packer, *Knowing God* (Downers Grove: InterVarsity Press, 1973), 137.

6. John 14:21a

7. Daniel Heimbach, *True Sexual Morality* (Wheaton: Crossway, 2004), 189.

8. For more commands prohibiting bestiality, see Deuteronomy 27:21; Exodus 22:19; Leviticus 20:15–16.

9. Romans 13:1–2

10. Allen P. Ross, *Holiness to the Lord: A Guide to the Exposition of the Book of Leviticus* (Grand Rapids: Baker Academic, 2002), 339.

11. The Guardian, "Houston Officials Halt Plans to Open First US 'RobotBrothel,'" accessed September 30, 2018, https://www.theguardian.com/us-news/2018/sep/30/houston-robot-brothel-plan-halted.

12. American Psychiatric Association, *Desk Reference to the Diagnostic Criteria for the DSM-5* (Arlington: American Psychiatric Publishing, 2013), 337.

13. Gary Thomas, "50 Problems with Grey," accessed February 12, 2015, http://www.garythomas.com/50shades/.

14. This is based off the English Standard Version translation of 1 Corinthians 13:4–6.

15. Dannah Gresh and Dr. Juli Slattery, *Pulling Back the Shades* (Chicago: Moody Publishers, 2014), 77.

16. Juli Slattery, "Guidelines for Christian Sex," *Today's Christian Woman*, accessed October 2013, https://www.todayschristianwoman.com/articles/2013/october/christian-sex-guidelines.html.

Chapter 7: Why Sexual Sin Is Sin: Sex Is Convenantal

1. *The Princess Bride*, directed by Rob Reiner (20th Century Fox, 1987), VHS.

2. John Piper, "Sex and the Single Man," *Desiring God*, accessed January 18, 2021, https://www.desiringgod.org/messages/sex-and-the-single-man.

3. Timothy Keller and Kathy Keller, *The Meaning of Marriage* (New York: Dutton, 2011), 85.

4. *The Book of Common Prayer* (New York: Penguin Group, 2012), 311–20.

5. Wayne Grudem, "Grounds for Divorce: Why I Now Believe There Are More Than Two," (lecture, The Evangelical Theological Society, San Diego, CA, November 21, 2019).

6. For those who wish to study 1 Corinthians 7 and remarriage in greater detail, I commend the book *God, Marriage, and Family* by Andreas J. Kostenberger and David W. Jones.

7. Glynn Harrison, *A Better Story: God, Sex, and Human Flourishing* (London: Inter-Varsity Press, 2017), 146.

8. Exodus 20:14; Deuteronomy 5:18; Matthew 19:18; Romans 13:9

9. Kevin DeYoung, *The Hole in Our Holiness* (Wheaton: Crossway, 2012), 110.

10. 1 Timothy 5:2 (ESV)

11. The Corinthians said a similar thing to Paul, which is why he engaged them in a conversation about what's permissible versus what's beneficial in 1 Corinthians 6:12–20.

12. Centers for Disease Control and Prevention, "STD Risk & Oral Sex—CDC Fact Sheet," accessed February 16, 2019, https://www.cdc.gov/std/healthcomm/stdfact-stdriskandoralsex.htm.

13. John Piper, "Is Oral Sex Okay?" Desiring God, accessed August 5, 2014, https://www.desiringgod.org/interviews/is-oral-sex-okay.

14. Juli Slattery, "What's OK in the Bedroom," Authentic Intimacy, accessed November 15, 2016, https://www.authenticintimacy.com/resources/3499/whats-ok-in-the-bedroom.

15. John Piper, "Is it Sinful to Watch Porn with My Spouse?" Desiring God, accessed October 26, 2016, https://www.desiringgod. org/interviews/is-it-sinful-to-watch-porn-with-my-spouse.

Chapter 8: Why Sexual Sin Is Sin: Sex Is Fruitful

1. Mark 10:30 ESV
2. To learn more about the different types of birth control, read *Fearfully and Wonderfully Made: Christian Ethics and the Beginning of Human Life* by Dr. Megan Best, or read her article for the ERLC on "The Confusion about Contraceptives."
3. Job 31:15; Psalm 51:5; 139:13–16; Matthew 1:20
4. John Piper, "Is Permanent Birth Control a Sin," Desiring God, accessed November 27, 2019, https://www.desiringgod.org/ interviews/is-permanent-birth-control-a-sin.
5. Karen Swallow Prior, "Called to Childlessness: The Surprising Ways of God," ERLC, accessed November 27, 2019, https://erlc.com/resource-library/articles/called-to-childlessness-the-surprising-ways-of-god.
6. Deuteronomy 32:39; Job 12:10; 33:4
7. Diane Langberg, *Suffering and the Heart of God* (Greensboro, NC: New Growth Press, 2015), 146–53.
8. A helpful resource that can aid you in your journey of processing an abortion is *Surrendering the Secret* by Pat Layton.

Chapter 9: Why Sexual Sin Is Sin: Sex Is Selfless

1. 1 Corinthian 7:3–4
2. Daniel R. Heimbach, *True Sexual Morality* (Wheaton: Crossway Books, 2004), 165.
3. Darby Strickland, "Sexual Abuse in Marriage," CCEF, accessed November 16, 2019, https://www.ccef.org/sexual-abuse-in-marriage/.
4. In marriage, marital rape can occur where the wife is the perpetrator of forced sex, but more often, the wife is the victim, not the husband.
5. 1 Corinthians 13:5
6. 1 Thessalonians 4:3–7
7. 1 Timothy 2:9–10; 1 Peter 3:3–6; and 1 Corinthians 11:2–16 are three notable passages that discuss women's clothing.
8. 1 Timothy 3:15
9. 1 Timothy 2:9–10 ESV
10. Regarding 1 Timothy 2:9–10, I am indebted to Courtney Veasey and our conversations regarding her doctoral thesis, *A Lexical*

Semantic Study of καταστολή *and Its Function Within 1 Timothy 2:9,*
where she interprets the word seen as "apparel" in verse 9 as "proper
restraint" and argues that directives about clothing should be understood from this overall idea of self-control.
11. Matthew 12:33

Chapter 10: Why Sexual Sin Is Sin: Sex Is Symbolic

1. Romans 5:8
2. John 14:2–3
3. Luke 22:18
4. Allen P. Ross, *Recalling the Hope of Glory* (Grand Rapids: Kregel
Academic & Professional, 2006), 394.
5. 1 Corinthians 6:20; Galatians 3:13; Ephesians 1:7
6. Corinthians 11:26

Chapter 11: How to Identify the Roots of Your Sexual Struggles

1. Jeremiah 17:9
2. Charlotte Brontë, *Jane Eyre* (New York: Bantam Dell, 2003), 342.
3. Ibid.
4. Ibid.

Chapter 12: Action Steps for Fighting Sin

1. This Spiritual Laxative Principle is based on Thomas Chalmers'
sermon "The Expulsive Power of a New Affection."
2. Romans 13:14
3. Colossians 3:5

Chapter 13: How to Go from Emotionally Unhealthy to Healthy

1. Psalm 147:3
2. Examples of such commands include Joshua 1:9; Romans
12:9–10; Ephesians 4:26; 5:25.
3. Colossians 3:1–2
4. Romans 8:29
5. Dr. Dan B. Allender and Dr. Tremper Longman III, *The Cry of the
Soul* (Colorado Springs: NavPress, 1994), 34.
6. C. S. Lewis, *The Screwtape Letters* (New York: HarperSanFrancisco,
1942), 45.

7. A. W. Tozer, *The Knowledge of the Holy* (New York: HarperOne, 1961), 1.

8. Charitie Lees Bancroft, "Before the Throne of God Above," public domain.

9. Edward Welch, "Strong Emotions; Extreme Confidence" CCEF, accessed July 29, 2020, https://www.ccef.org/strong-emotions-extreme-confidence/.

10. Paul David Tripp, *Instruments in the Redeemer's Hands* (Phillipsburg, NJ: P&R Publishing, 2002), 54.

Chapter 14: How to Walk Alongside Others in the Battle

1. John 15:4–5

2. John 15:16 ESV

3. John Flavel, "The Method of Grace" in *The Whole Works of John Flavel*, vol. 2 (London: Baynes, 1820) 438, quoted in Diane Mandt Langberg, *In Our Lives First* (Jenkintown, PA: Diane Langberg PhD & Associates, 2014), 25.

4. During my shingles season, I listened to the men's round-table series *A Man and His Work* from Grace Community Church in Greenville, South Carolina, which informed my thinking about rest, work, recreation, and escapism.

5. Thanks to Sara Young for this description!

Chapter 15: How God Heals Our Brokenness

1. Walter Bauer, *A Greek-English Lexicon of the New Testament and Other Early Christian Literature*, rev. and ed. Frederick W. Danker, 3rd ed. (Chicago: University of Chicago Press: 2000), 552.

2. Matt Mason, "This Is Our Story" (sermon, The Church at Brook Hills, Birmingham, AL, May 17, 2020).

3. Sam Allberry, *7 Myths about Singleness* (Wheaton: Crossway, 2019), 67.

4. C. S. Lewis, *The Screwtape Letters* (New York: HarperSanFrancisco, 1942), 8.

5. Mark Dever, *What Is a Healthy Church?* (Wheaton: Crossway, 2005), 40.

6. Thanks to John Butterfield for this tidbit of wisdom and for helping me be more strategic about discipleship.

7. Matt Mason, "Grasping the Basics, Again" (sermon, The Church at Brook Hills, Birmingham, Alabama, September 29, 2019).

8. Warren W. Wiersbe, *The Wiersbe Bible Commentary: Old Tesatment*, 2nd ed. (David C. Cook, 2007), 145.

9. Jonathan Edwards, "Resolutions," *A Jonathan Edwards Reader*, ed. John E. Smith, Harry S. Stout, and Kenneth P. Minkema (New Haven: Yale Nota Bene, 2003), 275.

10. Zephaniah 3:17; Matthew 11:29

11. Matthew 11:28–30

12. Revelation 21:1–6

13. John Newton, "Amazing Grace! How Sweet the Sound" (No. 330) in *Baptist Hymnal* (Nashville: Broadman & Holman Publishers, 1991).

Appendix B: A Word on Sex Addiction

1. The Augustine Fellowship, "Characteristics of Sex and Love Addiction," Sex and Love Addicts Anonymous, accessed February 20, 2020, https://slaafws.org/download/core-files/Characteristics-of-Sex-Love-Addiction.pdf.

2. Patrick Carnes, *Out of the Shadows: Understanding Sexual Addiction*, 3rd ed. (Center City, MN: Hazelden, 2001), 29–30.

3. Ibid., 14.

4. Marnie C. Ferree, *No Stones: Women Redeemed from Sexual Addiction*, 2nd ed. (Downers Grove, IL: InterVarsity Press, 2010), 51.

5. Edward Welch, *Addictions: A Banquet in the Grave* (Phillipsburg, NJ: P&R Publishing, 2001), 35.

6. Exodus 13:17

7. Joe S. McIlhaney and Freda McKissic Bush, *Hooked: The Brain Science on How Casual Sex Affects Human Development* (Chicago: Northfield Publishing, 2019), 26–28.

8. Dr. Mark R. Laaser, *Healing the Wounds of Sexual Addiction* (Grand Rapids: Zondervan, 2004), 150. Marnie C. Ferree, *No Stones: Women Redeemed from Sexual Addiction*, 2nd ed. (Downers Grove, IL: InterVarsity Press, 2010), 167.

9. Michael John Cusick, *Surfing for God* (Nashville: Thomas Nelson, 2012), 132. Marnie C. Ferree, *No Stones: Women Redeemed from Sexual Addiction*, 2nd ed. (Downers Grove, IL: InterVarsity Press, 2010), 52, 169–70.

10. This parallels Steps 5, 8, and 9 in the Twelve Steps of Sex Addicts Anonymous.

11. C. S. Lewis, *The Screwtape Letters* (New York: Harper SanFrancisco, 1942), 111.

12. John 15:5

13. Edward Mote, "My Hope Is Built on Nothing Less" (No. 459) in *Trinity Psalter Hymnal* (Orthodox Presbyterian Church and United Reformed Churches of North America, 2018).

14. Romans 6:17–18

Appendix C: A Word on Sexual Abuse

1. Darby Strickland, *Domestic Abuse: Recognize, Respond, Rescue* (Phillipsburg, NJ: P&R Publishing, 2018), 3.

2. Justin Holcomb and Lindsey Holcomb contain a helpful chapter with such lists in *Is It My Fault? Hope and Healing for Those Suffering Domestic Violence.*

3. Isaiah 53:4 ESV

4. J. Alec Motyer, *The Prophecy of Isaiah: An Introduction & Commentary* (Downers Grove, IL: IVP Academic, 1993), 428–30.

Appendix D: A Word on Trauma

1. Diane Langberg, *Suffering and the Heart of God: How Trauma Destroys and Christ Restores* (Greensboro: New Growth Press, 2015), 234.

2. Ibid., 149.

3. Darby Strickland, *Becoming a Church that Cares Well for the Abused*, ed. Brad Hambrick (Nashville: B&H Publishing, 2019), 36–37.

4. Ibid., 40.

5. Jennifer Michelle Greenberg, *Not Forsaken* (Charlotte, NC: The Good Book Company, 2019), 189.

6. Diane Langberg, *Suffering and the Heart of God: How Trauma Destroys and Christ Restores* (Greensboro, NC: New Growth Press, 2015), 146–53.

7. Revelation 21:8

8. Revelation 21:27

9. Revelation 21:23

10. Revelation 21:3c–5a